D. Wright, Jr.
18–1919

Clare N. Stannard
1919–1920

Dr. Harry C. Brown
1920–1921

Harold W. Moore
1921–1922

Finlay L. MacFarland
1922–1923

Harry A. Marr
1923–1924

H. Brown Cannon
1924–1925

Ralph B. Mayo
1925–1926

rt S. Sands
4–1935

Lawrence C. Blunt
1935–1936

W. W. Grant
1936–1937

Lewis J. Todhunter
1937–1938

William E. Russell
1938–1939

Guy W. Faller
1939–1940

L. Ward Bannister
1940–1941

Frank P. Spratlen, Jr.
1941–1942

am Grant
0–1951

P. Hicks Cadle
1951–1952

Mortimer Stone
1952–1953

John G. McMurtry
1953–1954

George M. Hopfenbeck
1954–1955

Milton E. Bernet
1955–1956

Robert L. Stearns
1956–1957

Ray Jenkins
1957–1958

r K. Koch
6–1967

Robert H. McWilliams
1967–1968

John H. Amesse
1968–1969

Richard M. Davis
1969–1970

Peter D. Bowes
1970–1971

John J. Vance
1971–1972

Earl S. Stone
1972–1973

C. Howard Kast
1973–1974

erne Hart
82–1983

Gary F. McMahon
1983–1984

Kermit L. Darkey
1984–1985

Junius F. Baxter
1985–1986

Robert K. Timothy
1986–1987

David E. Fleming
1987–1988

Richard L. Anderson
1988–1989

Garth C. Grissom
1989–1990

J. O'Connell
98–1999

James C. Mack
1999–2000

Joan H. Bristol
2000–2001

R. J. Ross
2001–2002

Richard W. Metcalfe
2002–2003

Steven C. Mast
2003–2004

Robert J. Kapelke
2004–2005

Rebecca A. Mallory
2005–2006

Denver Rotary Club 31 Presidents

THE FIRST 100 YEARS

Denver Rotary Celebrates a Century of Service

ROTARY CLUB OF DENVER

ROTARY INTERNATIONAL

1911   2011

A CENTURY OF SERVICE

THE
DONNING COMPANY
PUBLISHERS

THE FIRST 100 YEARS

Denver Rotary Celebrates a Century of Service

BY ROSEMARY FETTER

This book is dedicated to Club 31 Denver Rotarians, past, present, and future.
Your commitment, sense of honor, and good works have made both
the city and the world community a better place.

To Rex,
Best wishes,
Rosemary Fetter

OUR SPONSORS

GOLD
Mountain States Employers Council
National Western Stock Show
Qwest

SILVER
William H. and Suzanne Davis Hornby
Van Gilder Insurance Corporation

BRONZE

100 Years of Service Above Self
  Congratulations, Jim & Bev Warner
9Health Fair, *Trainers for Rotary health fairs worldwide*
American Zang Education Preservation Foundation, Inc.
  The Rod Greiner Family—DKI President 1998–99
Arthur P. Roy, Colorado Court of Appeals
Beverly S. Hutter Jr. "Bev"
  Hutter+Eurobath
C. Grant Wilkins
  Club President 78/79—5450 DG 84/85—RI Director 93/95
C. Howard Kast
  Club President 1973–74 & District Governor 1976–77
Carleton G. Lindsay
Carol Duncan and Jay Yake
  The Duncan Team—Keller Williams Realty
Carolyn Smith and Gretchen S. Kneen
  In Honor of Preston Smith
Davis Graham & Stubbs LLP
  Dale Harris & Robert Harry
Denver Kids, Inc.
  Donna Hultin & Glenna Norvelle
Denver Machine Shop—Since 1916
  Lee, Jim, Eric and Scott White
Frank D. Lawrence
  DRCF President 2010–2011
Frederick L. Grover, MD, Aragon/Gonzalez-Giusti Chair
  Dept. of Surgery, CU School of Medicine
Gerald M. Quiat
J. Michael O'Connell
  President, 1998–99
James C. Mack
  Club President, 1999–2000
Jim & Scotty Wilkins
  Rotary Club President 1994–95
Jim Cohig
John E. Lucken
  Consulting Geologist
John R. Klug
Joseph G. Hodges Jr.
  Attorney at Law
Larry Gloss
  Gloss & Company
Margaret Fomer, PhD—Executive Director
  Denver Girls 1987–93; Denver Boys 1992–93; DKI 1993–01
Marlene Wilkins
Nick Muller, for my Grandsons
  Pete & Nicko, future Rotarians!
Nina and Jim McGibney
One Hundred Years of Service Above Self,
  Hank & Joan Strauss

P. Douglas and Holly McLemore
  Denver Rotary President 2010–11
Peter J. Wall
Phil Heinschel
  Club Secretary 1996–97
Phillip "Phil" Pankey
  In Honor of Ralph Hverploeg, M.D.
Rev. R. J. Ross
  Club President 2001–02
Rich Harris, The Harris Law Firm, P.C.
  Proud to Partner with Rotary
Richard Anderson
Richard W. Metcalfe, DDS, MS
  Club President 2002–2003
Robert G. Heiserman II, in Honor of my Father, a 1968
  Charter Member & President Ashburn Rotary, Georgia
Robert H. Lowdermilk
  Club President—2008-Six Days
Robert J. Kapelke
  President, 2004–05
Robert K. Timothy
  Club President 1986–87
Roger L. Kinney
Roland R. Thornton
  Club President 2009–2010
Roy Berkeley
  Berkeley-Lainson
Sandy Adams, CPA
Seth L. Patterson
  Centennial Year Club President, 2011–2012
Skip Ahern
  Charter Realty Group, LLC
Steve Mast, Club President 2003–04 &
  Darlene Mast, Club Executive Director since 2004
Sue Anschutz-Rodgers
Sue Fox, Club President 2008–2009
  Susan R. Fox, Attorney at Law
Ted and Lana Friedman
  Friedman Realty Associates
The Denver Athletic Club
Thomas J. Butler
Trinity United Methodist Church
  Denver's First Church
UMB Bank Colorado, N.A.
  UMB High School Scholarship Program
William T. Diss
With Gratitude and Appreciation,
  Thank you Pete

Thank you to William (Bill) Hornby, Past President of the Rotary Club of Denver (1976–77) who penned and
spearheaded production of *A Club and a City* for Denver Rotary's 75th Anniversary Celebration in 1986.

The Donning Company Publishers
184 Business Park Drive, Suite 206
Virginia Beach, VA 23462

Steve Mull, General Manager
Barbara B. Buchanan, Office Manager
Richard A. Horwege, Senior Editor
Lori Wiley, Graphic Designer
Priscilla Odango, Imaging Artist
Katie Gardner, Project Research Coordinator
Tonya Hannink, Marketing Specialist
Pamela Engelhard, Marketing Advisor

Cathleen Norman, Project Director

Library of Congress Cataloging-in-Publication Data

Fetter, Rosemary.
    The first 100 years : Denver Rotary celebrates a century of service / by
Rosemary Fetter.
        p. cm.
    Includes bibliographical references and index.
    ISBN 978-1-57864-698-2 (hbk. : alk. paper)
1. Denver Rotary Club (Denver, Colo.) 2. Businesspeople—Colorado—
Denver—Societies, etc. 3. Civic improvement—Colorado—Denver. I. Title.
II. Title: Denver Rotary celebrates a century of service.
    HF5001.R82D464 2011
    369.5'20978883—dc23
                                        2011031802

Printed in the USA at Walsworth Publishing Company

TABLE OF CONTENTS

FOREWORD
by Governor John Hickenlooper

When I came West, I originally planned to work as a geologist. After I became unemployed, I opened up Denver's first restaurant and brewpub in the 1888 J. S. Brown Mercantile Building on Wynkoop Street. Although I had no previous experience in the restaurant business, I found myself restoring and renovating one of the city's historic buildings, an early effort toward the revival of Lower Downtown.

The project piqued my interest in local history. I soon realized that any history of Denver is a history of Denver business, beginning with the merchants who came here during the gold rush and stayed to build a city. As they flourished, they built a diverse economy that has led us successfully into the future.

Although more than one hundred thousand people passed through Denver on their way to the goldfields, the city would never have grown but for a handful of innovative businessmen like David Moffat, John Evans, Sr., and William Newton Byers, who garnered support to build a transportation system that linked Denver to the rest of the country. Thanks to their efforts, the city became the rail hub of the Rockies.

During the past century and a half, Denver has progressed from an isolated mining town without much promise to the diverse and culturally rich city we enjoy today. On many occasions, Denverites have relied on business leadership during times of crisis, whether financial, social or inflicted by nature. A great number of these business owners and managers have been members of Denver Rotary.

Since the founding of Denver Club 31 in 1911, Rotarian contributions to the city have been innumerable, both individually and as a group. Supporting Mayor Robert Speer, Rotarians helped to create our "City Beautiful," with parks and tree-lined thoroughfares, and developed water resources to green the dusty plains. Rotarians supported the creation of Rocky Mountain National Park and the Emily Griffith Opportunity School. They campaigned for better roads and highways, museums and other cultural facilities, and offered financial and emotional support for children in need. Countless other projects have been vital to the welfare of the community.

As a Rotarian for the past twenty years, I've always been impressed by the way the club exemplifies the spirit of collaboration that creates a successful business environment. Focusing on "Service above Self," Rotary stresses cooperation, never allowing partisan politics or personal interest to get in the way of group achievement.

Rotarians are the most dedicated volunteers, always willing to help. Working as a team, they accomplish miracles, not only in the city's neighborhoods but internationally, from eradicating polio and providing clean water for third world countries to mentoring kids to keep them in school and out of trouble. They connect with one another worldwide, and together they make things happen.

As only the thirty-first of more than thirty-four thousand clubs worldwide, Denver Rotarians can be proud of their accomplishments over the past century and know that their efforts have truly made a difference.

Congratulations on one hundred years of service! We look forward to many more!

John Hickenlooper

INTRODUCTION

by Tom "Dr. Colorado" Noel

It all started back in 1905, when a Chicago lawyer named Paul Harris made the interesting suggestion that business should serve the community and not the other way around. He also believed in an organization where friendships and common interests dull the edge of cutthroat competition, provide an atmosphere that nourishes entrepreneurs and offer endless opportunities to do good works. With this in mind, he founded the first Rotary Club, which spread to thirty other U.S. cities in the next six years.

The possibility of such a club in Denver captured the imagination of typewriter salesman Gratton E. Hancock. In October 1911, Hancock gathered together a few friends and made his sales pitch. Rather than catering to the Capitol Hill tycoons like other men's clubs, he explained that Denver Rotary would be the purview of the average business leader. Membership would be limited to "proprietors, partners or corporate officers."

Along with the creation of business friendships, the goal would be community service, and the motto "Service Above Self" would be a serious commitment, not just a catch phrase. Some of the first members had already been involved with Mayor Robert Speer's "City Beautiful" movement, the ambitious effort to turn dusty, drab Denver into "Paris on the Platte."

On December 9, 1911, Club 31 received its charter. Within the decade, Denver Rotary had sponsored clubs around the state and in Wyoming and New Mexico.

During the next century, Rotarians as individuals, and as a club, were involved with every aspect of Denver's development, from charitable organizations and civic improvements to real estate development,

highway construction, sports and entertainment and higher education. The club counted among its members such heavy hitters as architect Temple Buell, U.S. Supreme Court Justice Byron "Whizzer" White, aviator Elrey P. Jeppesen, attorney Stephen Hart, banker Roger Knight, Jr., social reformer Edgar Wahlburg, and entertainer/philosopher Pete Smythe.

Denver Rotary's efforts have made the city and the world a better place, which is the highest compliment any organization can receive. From Denver Kids, which has changed the lives of thousands, to Polio Plus, a program that is expected to eradicate polio worldwide by 2012, Denver Rotary has always been willing to pitch in and lend a hand when the need arises. Through their Centennial project, which will support history and social studies education statewide, Club 31 will continue to give back to the community as it has for the past century.

Rosemary Fetter, a veteran Denver historian and writer, tells the club's heartening story in this book. It celebrates Denver Rotary's one hundred years of service and explains why we should all look forward to many more!

Thomas J. Noel

> *An organization that is wholly selfish cannot last long. If we, as a Rotary Club, expect to survive and grow, we must do some things to justify our existence. We must perform a civic service.*
>
> —Donald M. Carter, 1906

This view of downtown Denver at the intersection of Colfax Avenue and Broadway, circa 1910, shows the old City Hall and the Daniels and Fisher Tower in the background. Photo courtesy Denver Public Library Western History Department.

CHAPTER I

Rotary Comes to Denver
1911–1925

THE SETTING

In many ways, Denver was still a small town with big ambitions in late 1911, when the first local Rotary meeting took place. The city had entered the twentieth century on tiptoe, glad to be alive after its first few turbulent decades. Founded on a gamble for gold and maintained by railroad and land speculation, Denver remained largely dependent on precious metals and foreign capital until the Depression of 1893 shook the system to its financial core. This disaster crushed the state's silver mining industry, creating a financial panic. Banks failed, construction froze and Denver's streets overflowed with legions of the unemployed. As heavy industry and agriculture began to replace mining as the state's economic base, Denver turned to entrepreneurs like brewers Adolph Coors and Philip H. Zang, and rubber products manufacturer Charles Gates, realizing (not for the last time) that diversification would be key to survival. These new kings of industry, or their progeny, would eventually join a new organization called the Denver Rotary.

By the early 1900s, the city was back on its feet, still struggling to overcome the raw frontier town image created by Eastern journalists and Ned Buntline's ten-cent paperbacks. As the National Western Stock Growers Association built a six-thousand-seat arena to host the January stock show, Denver waffled between promoting and repudiating its Wild West heritage. When city boosters, headed by future Rotarians Charles Franklin and Mayor Robert Speer, scored the 1908 Democratic Convention, it went a long way toward gilding the lily. That year, hoping to put the city on the map, Denverites built an ultramodern auditorium to accommodate the doomed Dems and their free silver candidate, Williams Jennings Bryan. The neoclassical showplace became Mayor Robert Speer's first major architectural coup.

Zang Brewery, seen here in 1905, numbered among many prosperous businesses in early Denver. Photo courtesy Rosemary Fetter.

The Daniels and Fisher Department Store Tower built in 1911, was reputedly one of the tallest structures in the country. Photo courtesy Denver Public Library Western History Department.

Another City Beautiful project, the Civic Center Park and the Pioneer Monument and Fountain, debuted in 1911, the latter once again paying tribute to the rip-roaring past. When sculptor Frederick MacMonnies tried to top the fountain with a bronze Indian, however, irate Denverites with long memories insisted on a figure of Kit Carson instead. In 1920, Rotarian Stephen Knight, grandfather of future club president Roger D. Knight, Jr., funded another bronze statue, the *Equestrian Indian*, which occupied a less conspicuous spot in Civic Center's Sculpture Garden.

As the nation's twenty-fifth largest city in 1911, Denver could boast one of the highest structures in the country, the Daniels and Fisher Tower. According to the most recent census, the city had a population of 213,381, a respectable gain of nearly 80,000 during the first decade of the new century. Like Chicago, the birthplace of Rotary International, Denver was a city of contrasts, with pollution, poverty, and deplorable slums within whiffing distance of Capitol Hill. Although Denverites owned at least three thousand automobiles, unpaved bumpy roads prevailed. Streetcars remained the lifeline of the middle class, permitting commuters to retreat to suburban communities like Park Hill, Highlands, Washington Park, South Denver, and Montclair, and, for those with heftier wallets, the new Country Club neighborhood in East Denver.

The Municipal Auditorium, a Speer administration triumph, welcomed the Democratic National Convention in 1908 and the Rotary International Convention in 1926. Photo courtesy Denver Public Library Western History Department.

The Knight-Campbell Music Company became one of the first businesses in the Denver Rotary family. Photo courtesy Denver Public Library Western History Department.

During the club's early years, luncheons were held at members' business establishments, such as Gates Rubber Company, shown here. Photo courtesy Denver Public Library Western History Department.

Businesses that would be around for decades were either starting out or expanding. For example, Charles Gates, Sr., one of Rotary's early movers and shakers, bought the Colorado Tire and Leather Company for $3,500 in 1911, building it over the next few decades into a leading national rubber products company. His first customers included showman Buffalo Bill Cody, who liked the company's halters so much that he became a chief promoter. Other blossoming enterprises included City Floral, Mountain States Telephone and Telegraph Company, Barnes Commercial College, the Knight-Campbell Music Company, and Robinson Dairy, the latter founded back in 1885. They would all be welcomed into the Rotary fold.

A NEW KIND OF CLUB

In 1911, Denver had no shortage of men's clubs. Private groups such as the Denver Country Club, the Denver Club, University Club, Cactus Club, and the Denver Athletic Club served a small segment of the population, catering mostly to the old guard and their male heirs. For the average CEO, however, friendships in the city could be difficult to achieve and maintain. The government often turned a blind eye toward unethical and "dog-eat-dog" business practices, keeping the big-city businessman constantly on guard. Rotary would afford a perfect opportunity for a Denver entrepreneur to enjoy the camaraderie and mutual trust he might find in a small town, supporting his fellows while serving the community and gaining a voice in local affairs.

Rotary International was founded in 1905 by Paul Harris, a Chicago lawyer, born in Wisconsin and raised in New England. His parents spent their final years in Denver, where as a young man, Harris worked as an actor at the People's Theater (Fifteenth Street Theater). He also was a reporter for *The Denver Post* and *Denver Times* and a cowboy on a ranch near Platteville. He later studied law, and became a lawyer in Chicago. In February 1905, Harris suggested to a group of four friends that they organize a club specifically for businessmen, with a membership limited to the "proprietor, partner or corporate officers," one person from each business or profession. Meetings would be held in rotation at each member's place of business, hence the name Rotary. Although business solicitation and partnerships had been the early emphasis, the idea of community service became more important as the club grew.

Busy Rotarians at Wichita Conference. From left to right: Past International President Russell F. Grenier, Father John Handly of Austin, Harry W. Stanley of Wichita, International Vice-President Albert H. Cornell, H. A. Olmsted of Dallas, and International Director Gratton E. Hancock. Photo courtesy Rotary International.

FOUNDING FATHERS

In Denver, Gratton E. Hancock, a thirty-nine-year-old manager for the Smith-Premier Typewriter Company became the father of a fledgling Rotary club. Born February 2, 1872, in Syracuse, New York, location of the Smith-Premier headquarters and the origin of many early Denver Rotarians, Hancock had been raised in his grandparents' home like Paul Harris. As a youth, Hancock won fame as a master cyclist, a member of the prestigious Century Club of cyclists, and first winner of the grueling *Syracuse Herald* Road Race in 1892.

Although he lived in Denver only a few years, Hancock dived into the social and business life of the community, joining the Denver Chamber of Commerce, the Advertising Club and the Masonic Order. As superintendent of Grace United Methodist Church Sunday School, he displayed a sense of humor that later became a Rotarian trademark. To keep students in attendance during the lazy days of summer, he issued the following notice in late July:

Satisfactory Sabbath School SUMMER SERVICE secures a scenic September sylvan session soon. Situate some shady spot and sing sweet songs. Shout shrill soprano sounds. Select several sensible Sunday School scholars and so spend session.

[Signed] Superintendent.

Denver Rotary Club founder Gratton E. Hancock. Photo courtesy Rotary International.

He also included a punch card for each Sunday in August with the notation: "Superintendent will punch one each Sunday when present. To those who are present at least eight Sundays of the nine, bring the card and have it punched, a suburban trolley ride will be given free. Date and place will be announced later."

GRATTON E. HANCOCK
Remington Typewriters
Denver Rotary Club

Get the
Other 10

Typewriter salesman Gratton E. Hancock used his business card to solicit membership in Denver Rotary. Photo courtesy Denver Rotary Club.

If Hancock used the same technique to keep Rotary members in attendance, any evidence has been lost to history.

In July 1911, while on a business trip to Salt Lake City, Gratton Hancock met the secretary of that city's Rotary during "a salt water float" with associates. When he returned to Denver, Hancock wrote a letter to Chesley R. Perry, secretary of the National Association of Rotary, asking whether Denver had such an organization and, if not, how to start one. On July 24, Perry sent a letter of encouragement and a brochure that outlined the organization's caveats: strict attendance requirements; fines rather than dues; membership from all professions and occupations, key players only; and freedom from politics, with the purpose of giving "moral and educational support to great questions of public influence."

Rotary founder Paul Harris wrote directly to Hancock on August 11: "So far as the altruistic side of our curriculum is concerned," he maintained, "we can as a National Rotary bring to bear the same insistent force in national matters that, as a local Rotary, we can on municipal matters. The force of a combined Rotary operated from all the large cities . . . would be almost beyond conception."

On October 14, 1911, at 12:15 p.m., Hancock and curio shop owner George Harris gathered a small informal group to discuss the possibility of forming a Rotary Club in Denver. Well-known city boosters, they were probably supporters of Mayor Robert Speer, who soon became a member. The first gathering included the following:

Denver Rotary Financial Secretary George Harris owned the Harris Curio Company at Seventeenth Street and Broadway. Photo courtesy Denver Public Library Western History Department.

Charles W. Franklin, fifty-three, an attorney born in Missouri. Franklin, who had served as the chairman of the 1908 Democratic National Convention committee, was described in his obituary as "a driving force behind bringing the DNC to Denver." As a Rotarian, he later drafted the club's original constitution and by-laws, which became a national model. Hancock later attributed Rotary's success during the early years to Franklin's "activity and enthusiasm." A delegate to the 1914 National Convention in Buffalo, he died suddenly after returning home, the first Denver Rotarian lost to death. The entire club stood at his eulogy, a gesture of respect that began a long tradition.

George Harris, forty, owned the G. M. Harris Curio Company on Seventeenth and Broadway. His business specialized in Navajo rugs/blankets (which Harris guaranteed were genuine) and Mexican and Japanese curios.

Robert Willison, forty-six, an architect and partner in Willison and Fallis, was born in Kilmarnock, Scotland. A member of the Colorado chapter of the A.I.A., Willison designed the Denver Municipal Auditorium, St. Cajetan's Catholic Church, and later the Oxford Hotel addition with Montana Fallis. The Denver building inspector from 1904 to 1910, he and Franklin were undoubtedly supporters of Speer's "City Beautiful" objectives.

Harry E. Barnes was an Ohio native and secretary of Barnes Commercial School, a family business founded by his brother, Elmer, in 1904. By 1917, the school boasted 160 typewriters, many of which were likely purchased from Hancock.

Sam Dutton was a native of New York like Hancock. A former employee of the Harvey Restaurant chain, Dutton was proprietor and later owner of the Albany Hotel, where early Rotary meetings and many activities of the 1926 International Rotary Convention would be held.

Arthur L. Chandler, American Multigraph Sales Company district manager, served as the club's first treasurer.

After the first successful meeting, Hancock sent a letter to potential members in an attempt to drum up enthusiasm. In the letter, he quoted Rotary's three major goals: "the promotion of the business interests of its members, the promotion of good fellowship and civic and commercial development of the city. . . ."

Sam Dutton, one of the original Denver Rotarians, operated the Albany Hotel at Seventeenth and Stout Streets, site of the club's first meetings. Photo courtesy Denver Public Library Western History Department.

ROBERT W. SPEER AND THE CITY BEAUTIFUL

Robert Walter Speer came to Colorado to recover from TB and stayed to become the most powerful mayor Denver has ever seen. Photo courtesy Tom Noel.

The most powerful mayor Denver has ever seen, the visionary Robert Walter Speer had a genius for politics coupled with charisma and bulldog determination, a combination that made for ardent supporters and bitter enemies. A self-proclaimed political "boss," an energetic city booster and an insightful leader, Speer transformed the dusty and uninviting mining and rail center into a modern city with verdant parks and gardens and a tree-lined boulevard and parkway system. As one of his friends said upon his death in 1918, "Denver is and always will be his monument."

Speer was born into a comfortable middle-class family on December 1, 1855, and for a short time attended Dickinson Seminary in Williamsport. At age twenty-three, like many tuberculosis sufferers, he relocated to Denver, where sunshine, dry air, and the pristine climate affected a miraculous cure. With a sunny disposition that matched his newfound health, he started out as a clerk selling carpets at Daniels and Fisher Department Store. Before long he became involved in real estate and joined developers of the prestigious Denver Country Club district, where he built his own home at 300 Humboldt Street. A budding politician with a finger in every pie, he was elected mayor in 1904, 1908, and 1916.

Although his methods have been questioned, Speer made countless contributions to Denver's development. An early environmentalist, he gave away 110,000 shade trees, created the Denver Mountain Parks system, and built many city parks, including Inspiration Point, with its three-hundred-mile panoramic view of the Rockies. He loved animals and birds and helped to create the Denver Museum of Natural History and modernize the Denver Zoo, which became a national model.

(During one speech, the enigmatic mayor once told astonished Rotarians that "animals, grain and vegetables have life and suffer when injured the same as any of us," a statement that may or may not have helped the zoo project.)

Speer loved beauty, and through his efforts came Denver's Civic Center and Greek Amphitheater, the reclamation of unsightly Cherry Creek and the creation of playgrounds for children all over the city. Coining the phrase, "Give while you live," he convinced Denver businessmen and fellow Rotarians to contribute financially to the city that brought them success. "Denver has been kind to most of us by giving to some health, to some wealth, to some happiness and to some a combination of all," he told the Chamber of Commerce in 1909. "We can pay part of this debt by making our city more attractive."

Architect Jacques B. Benedict designed the Sunken Gardens on Speer Boulevard near West High School, a City Beautiful improvement along Cherry Creek. Photo courtesy Denver Public Library Western History Department.

The creation of the Denver Park System was one of Speer's priorities. This 1918 view of Denver City Park shows the Colorado Museum of Natural History (now the Denver Museum of Nature and Science) in the background. The nearby Denver Zoo also ranked high on the list of mayoral pet projects. Photo courtesy Denver Public Library Western History Department.

"Rotary is a quality organization of quality men producing quality goods. Or, if professional, dispensing quality thought, word, and deed," he added. "Every member is active." In the letter, he underlined the word *quality* each time.

Encouraged by the response, Hancock called another meeting ten days later with Kansas City Rotarian Lee B. Mettler, who advised the group on the formation of a new club and, according to *The Rotarian* (first published in 1911), let them know how lucky they were to be Denver's first Rotarians. Hancock subsequently formed a temporary organization with twenty-seven members. At the third meeting, the new club elected a slate of officers, including:

President: Gratton E. Hancock
Vice President: Charles W. Franklin
Second Vice President: John T. Hunter (Advertising Manager, A. T. Lewis & Sons Dry Goods)
Secretary: Arthur L. Chandler
Treasurer: Harry M. Beatty
Financial Secretary: George M. Harris
Statistician: William J. Pete
Sergeant-at-Arms: John J. Jacobs.

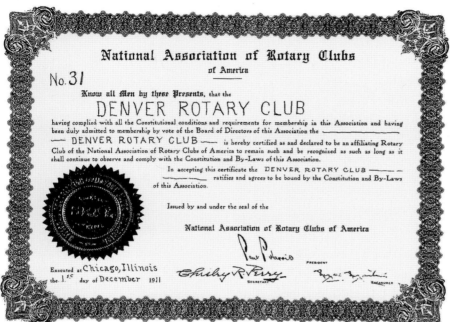

Denver Rotary Club 31 was chartered on December 1, 1911. The National Association formally recognized Club 31 on December 9, 1911. Photo courtesy Denver Rotary Club.

By November 2, Denver Rotary had formally organized and sent off a list of forty charter members to Chicago. The National Organization issued Charter No. 31 to the Denver Rotary Club on December 9, 1911.

According to an article Hancock produced for the club's national publication, *The Rotarian*, in 1917, "The club prospered from the start and was assisted materially in the first few months by the very valuable advice of Paul P. Harris." Apparently Harris took a special interest in the Denver group's development, possibly because of his early association with the city.

In the same article, Hancock wrote, "The Denver Rotary Club early in its career affiliated with the National Organization. Like many of the early clubs, there was a motive in its organization, and mentioned in the objects of the club which was soon to be eliminated—the promotion of business interests of its members." In an address to the club, which Hancock stated took place on December 6, he advised: "If there are any members whose ideas permit the predominating of Self rather than Service, this Club is the wrong place for them, as sooner or later they will find themselves out of sorts with their surroundings."

By the following year, membership had risen to seventy-five and Denver Rotary was on its way. After serving only four months as president, Hancock transferred to Salt Lake City in 1912, where he remained for the next year and a half. Jesse Wheelock, director of Northwestern Life Insurance Company, took over as president.

The club founder returned to Denver in 1914, having served as associate editor of *The Rotarian* the previous year. He became an International Rotary director in 1915, continuing to report on Denver events to the national publication until 1917.

EARLY PROJECTS

Answering Mayor Speer's challenge to give to the city, Denver Rotary became involved in civic affairs early in the game. According to a 1912 notice in the *Denver Chamber of Commerce Bulletin*, "The work of their Good Roads Committee is certainly to be commended. At a recent meeting, they had, as their guests, county commissioners from five adjoining counties. A fund of several hundred dollars was subscribed to the counties with the understanding that a like amount or more would be given by each county for the purpose of improving the roads leading to and from Denver." The same bulletin commended Rotary's work in the legislature, "in connection with the Tunnel, Good Roads and Immigration Bill."

As it turned out, the Progressive reformers ousted Speer and took control in 1912, the first year of initiative and referendum in Colorado. Denver women (who had won the vote in 1893) took a more active part in the election, and social issues like eight-hour workday for women and establishment of a juvenile court system in Colorado's larger cities took priority. Still, Denver Rotarians continued their efforts on behalf of better roadways and met with some success. As a result of Denver Rotarian efforts, in particular Jesse M. Wheelock and T. C. Hitchings, the legislature appropriated $1.5 million to improve roads in Colorado, while the warden of the state penitentiary agreed to use free prison labor. Another Denver Rotary goal, completion of the Moffat Tunnel project would not be accomplished until 1928.

An early Rotary Meeting, August 1913, shows men with musical instruments. In the front row, Rotarian Louis C. McClure holds a sign reading "McClure, L. C., Commercial Photographer." Photo courtesy Denver Public Library Western History Department.

23

The same Chamber of Commerce bulletin also noted a guest speaker at the Rotary's luncheon, a Denverite named Stanley McGuiness, who had spent several months in California and subsequently made comparisons between Denver and Los Angeles. Although the speaker found the two cities alike in certain amenities, he felt that the most valuable lessons Denver could learn from Los Angeles were "unity in the community in all matters affecting the general interest of the city" and "the care

In 1915–16, the club provided funds to help the Sunshine Rescue Mission at Eighteenth and Larimer Streets, where Rotarian Jim Goodhart served as superintendent. Photo courtesy Denver Public Library Western History Department.

of Los Angeles newspapers in minimizing any unfavorable mistakes or occurrences on the part of public officials."

The first club of its kind for Denver businessmen, Rotary had recruited 165 members by the time the Kiwanis and Optimist Clubs formed in 1916, followed by the Denver Lions Club in 1917. Before 1920, Denver Rotary would plant the seed for several Rotary clubs throughout the region. Together with Pueblo Rotary No. 43, founded separately on June 1, 1912, Denver sponsored the first new Colorado club, Rotary Club of Colorado Springs (originally the Rotary Club of the Pikes Peak Region) on May 1, 1916. In Colorado, Rotary Club of Greeley (1917); Boulder; Trinidad; Grand Junction; and Sheridan and Casper, Wyoming (all in 1919); Littleton (1922), Brighton (1935), Englewood (1937), and Aurora (1954) also would be added to the list.

Apparently the first Rotary meetings were informal, as reported in the December 7, 1961 *Mile High Keyway* by the man who was, at the time, the Denver club's oldest living member, Frank McLister. "Our early-day meetings were sometimes held at noon and sometimes in the evenings to better accommodate the membership. . . . We depended on each other for fun and entertainment and craft talks (where the members talked about their own businesses)," he fondly recalled. "One of the first meetings I remember was in the Grill Room of the Albany Hotel. In the center of the room was a large tile pool filled with Rocky Mountain trout. After the song and prayer we were each provided a fish net and told to select our trout . . . one of our members slipped and fell into the pool, to the consternation of the trout."

Rotarians liked music, and apparently sang at every meeting for several decades. According to *A Club and A City* by Bill Hornby, written for Denver Rotary's seventy-fifth anniversary, the early minutes are full of references to inter-city meetings, Ladies Nights and Father-Daughter dinners. Milton Burnet, 1955–56 president and unofficial club historian, noted in 1970 that picnics at Elitch Gardens began as early as August 31, 1917. A clipping with a series of cartoons depicted Rotarians at play, a.k.a. "Brown Cannon takes a header in the Fat Man's Race," and "Bill Cocks was on first for the Leans."

To ensure that members had joined for altruistic rather than strictly social reasons, the club stressed attendance along with the recruitment and financing of Denver delegates to national Rotary conventions. Important guests occasionally dropped in or

Children's Hospital at 2221 Downing Street, completed in 1917, was among the many charities supported by Denver Rotary. Photo courtesy Denver Public Library Western History Department.

served as guest speakers, like the Evangelist Billy Sunday and even Russian revolutionary Leon Trotsky, who spoke May 22, 1919, at the annual Stag Night on the Rotary Club of Petrograd. Denver Rotary ended its first decade with 210 members.

Despite the admonition to refrain from politics, Rotarians were very much involved with local affairs. In 1916, an article in *The Rotarian* by Hancock applauded the re-election (after a four-year hiatus) of Rotary's "loan member" Robert Speer, who pledged a "business administration," and chose Rotarian W. F. R. Mills, manager of parks and improvements, to head the cabinet. The election eliminated the commission form of government and reestablished the 1904 "Speer Charter" which gave Denver one of the most powerful mayoral offices in the country. When various business organizations were asked to select a councilman to serve during the first year, Denver Rotary chose Jesse Wheelock. At a banquet following the election, the Denver club promised its unequivocal support of Speer's efforts to "beautify and enrich the city." As it turned out, the mayor became a victim of the flu epidemic and died in May 1918. Mills served as mayor until 1919, followed by Dewey Bailey from 1919 to 1923.

At first, Denver Rotary lent most of its support to the charities and causes espoused by members. In 1915–16, the club provided a large sum to support the Sunshine Rescue Mission at 1820 Larimer Street, operated by Rotarian Jim Goodhart. Rotary also directed funds toward the Federation of Charities, a forerunner of Community Chest/United Way, administered by Denver Rotary's second president, Jesse Wheelock. Children's Hospital, a favorite project of *Denver Post* publishers Fred Bonfils and Harry Tammen, also received support.

THE ROTARY WURLITZER

A particular source of pride for music-loving Rotarians and one of its first major contributions to the city, a $50,000 state-of-the-art Wurlitzer organ debuted in 1917 at the Denver Municipal Auditorium. Speer had apparently set aside $50,000 for the organ before he left his second term of office, but the money had been spent in other ways. Denver Rotary subsequently raised approximately half the cost, although

The Wurlitzer organ in the Denver Municipal Auditorium was the pride of Denver Rotary. Photo courtesy Denver Public Library Western History Department.

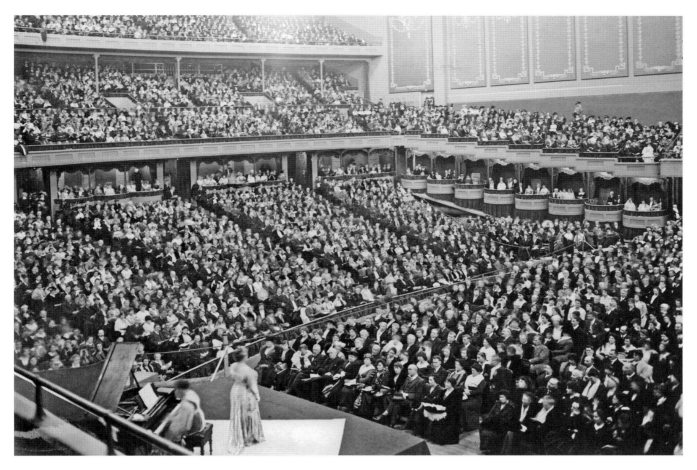

according to his obituary in the *Denver Times*, Speer contributed $30,000 of his own money. At a benefit concert to raise funds for the organ, on January 31, 1917, internationally renowned Ernestine Schumann-Hink, a fifty-year-old Wagnerian contralto, performed selections from Bach, Beethoven, Schumann, and Strauss at the Auditorium. The program cover featured a photo of the soloist in a feathered hat, above an ad for Meadow Gold Butter. Several other ads placed by Rotarians shored up the publication, including the Denver Rubber Tire Company, the Hoff-Schroeder Cafeteria, Mountain Motors Company at 25 Colfax (touting "Packard rhythm"), and the Knight-Campbell Music Company, which at the time sold windup record players. The largest event in Denver Rotary history up to that time, the benefit drew more than twelve thousand attendees and garnered approximately $5,000. Having raised enough to finally purchase the organ, the club made Mme. Schumann-Hink (who would later become the Hollywood prototype for buxom opera singers) an honorary Rotarian.

More than twelve thousand people attended a benefit to raise funds for the Wurlitzer, highlighted by a concert by opera star Ernestine Schumann-Hink. Photo courtesy Denver Public Library Western History Department.

WORLD WAR I PROJECTS AND AFTERMATH

Rotary priorities changed after April 6, 1917, when the United States entered World War I. A report to Rotary International on October 2, 1918, details Denver's Liberty Loan Campaigns, in which four hundred men and an unspecified number of women organized along military lines to solicit subscriptions throughout the city. As a sign of the times, the lead unit, called the "Flying Squadron" also was charged with "looking carefully into all reports from team members relative to pro-German or other unpatriotic remarks" or criticism of the government. "If further investigation warranted it," the individual's name would be turned over to the Secret Service. Since Denver had a large German population at the time, the team must have kept busy.

Intelligence work aside, other war projects included the creation of a War Chest for the Y.M.C.A. and the Red Cross and a combined War Camp Community Recreation Fund and Y.W.C.A. campaign. The quotas were $125,000 for Y.M.C.A., $35,000 for Y.W.C.A., and $20,000 for the War Camp Community Fund. The club would meet all goals and raise an additional $7,000. (Since the 2010 dollar had a purchasing power of $17 in 1917, this adds up to more than $3 million in modern currency.)

The club also held campaigns for Liberty Loan, War Savings Stamps and the collection of old clothes and shoes. On a more personal note, Denver Rotary also helped to provide lodging, clothing, and meals for new recruits and entertained 184 soldiers from Fort Logan at Thanksgiving and 175 at the Argonaut Hotel on Christmas. In addition, the club allocated $1,000 salary and expenses for six months to Jim Goodhart, who represented the Denver Rotary Club and the city under the Y.M.C.A. in France.

Rotarians often provided lodging and meals for troops during World War I. Photo courtesy Denver Public Library Western History Department.

The combination of World War I and the 1918 flu epidemic, which struck Denver particularly hard, inspired the city to retreat back into its shell once the "Yanks and Jerrys" fired their last shots. The city's population growth slowed along with the economy and showed no major gains until the next World War brought the military and their families to the city. A brief downtown building boom occurred from 1926 to 1927 with the addition of the Republic Building, the Security Building, Midland Savings, the Cosmopolitan Hotel, and Continental Oil Building to the city skyline.

Management/labor disputes at Denver Tramway became a major issue in 1919. Mayor Mills requested that a committee of five Rotarians (along with other businessmen) convene to find a solution to transit problems. The group, which included Frank Ashley, W. L. Loveland, Charles C. Gates, C. A. Kendrick, and H. Brown Cannon, made little progress. On August 5, 1921, an explosive confronta-

tion between strikers and strikebreakers left seven dead and fifty-two seriously wounded, with the violence continuing until federal troops arrived. Since Denver Rotary worked hand in glove with the mayor's office at the time, Rotary supported the new mayor, Dewey Bailey, who naturally blamed the workers.

In the early to mid-1920s, a wave of racial and religious bigotry settled over the state like a creeping fog. Led by 250-pound Denver physician John Galen Locke, Colorado became a hot spot for the white supremacist Ku Klux Klan, which was anti-Catholic, anti-Semitic and anti-African American. When the Klan took over the state, even five-term Rotarian Mayor Ben Stapleton joined the hooded brotherhood, for political rather than philosophical reasons. Rotarian Morrison Shafroth spoke out against the Klan and ran for attorney general and the U.S. Senate, but was defeated by Klan candidates.

Ben Stapleton eventually repudiated Klan affiliations and helped bring about Locke's downfall. His later administration was responsible for multiple civic improvements, including completion of the Denver Civic Center, Stapleton Airport, and expansion of the mountain parks system, including Red Rocks Park and Amphitheater.

Denverites celebrated when the Allies triumphed on November 11, 1918. Between World War I casualties and the influenza epidemic, the city was hard hit. Photo courtesy Denver Public Library Western History Department.

BOYS WORK AND THE MARKLEY SCHOLARSHIP

Denver Rotary continued its good work on the local scene. The club's involvement with Denver's boys began in summer 1921 with the appointment of a committee to study opportunities available for city boys on farms. On August 20, Denver Rotary's President H. W. More sent out a letter to members asking, "If you had to do it all over, would you get in more schooling than you did?"

In conjunction with Rotary International's one-day campaign to keep boys in school, members were asked to invite a boy to the next Thursday luncheon, particularly one who might be thinking about dropping out. The letter continued, "Let every Rotarian make it a point to drop some word to the boys seated at his table that will encourage the boys to believe that men who have succeeded in life believe in the boys getting as much education as they reasonably can."

The club supported Mayor Dewey Bailey during the Denver Tramway Strike of 1921. Photo courtesy Denver Public Library Western History Department.

In 1923, Denver Rotary formally began its service to young people in the community, although Denver Boys, Inc., would not come to fruition until after World War II. According to former executive secretary Wesley Towne, "At that time, there was much discussion as to whether we should contribute to some existing organizations or select a special activity and devote our energies to some particular work with boys. We began in a modest way to assist underprivileged boys in the high schools of Denver to buy adequate lunches, pay carfare, furnish shoes, clothing, and other needed items. The money given to these boys was a gift and they did not assume any obligation." That same year, Rotary established the Markley Scholarship and Achievement Award Program, named in honor of physician A. J. Markley, which provided thirty-six high school students with monetary support during the school year. This first step marked the beginning of Denver Rotary's continuing commitment to the city's youth

A coup of another kind occurred in June 1926, when Rotary International accepted Denver's bid to host the International Convention. One of the largest gatherings downtown Denver had seen up to that time, the celebration would make front-page news for weeks before and after the event.

Many Denver Rotarians attended the dedication of Rocky Mountain National Park in September 1919. Rotarians were great supporters of the Park and its primary advocate, naturalist Enos Mills. Photo courtesy Denver Public Library Western History Department.

This early photo shows Long's Peak in the background, the highest point in Rocky Mountain National Park. Photo courtesy Denver Public Library Western History Department.

A man is as great as the truth he speaks, as great as the help he gives, as great as the destiny he seeks and as great as the life he lives.

—C. E. Flynn, poet

Denver in the 1920s still had a small-town flavor. Photo courtesy Denver Public Library Western History Department.

CHAPTER II

The Club Expands
Between World Wars
1926–1940

ROTARY INTERNATIONAL COMES TO TOWN

By 1926, when Rotary International (RI) held its first Denver convention, the organization could proudly claim a presence in more than two thousand cities worldwide. Since fifteen-year-old Denver Rotary stood nowhere near the top of the list in terms of either population or prestige, snagging the conference had to be a remarkable achievement. Perhaps Enoch Josiah (Joe) Mills, younger brother of naturalist Enos Mills, helped pave the way in 1922. A born promoter, Mills had traveled to the RI Convention in Los Angeles to solicit support for a 1925 Convention in Estes Park, which still did not have its own Rotary Club. Plans fell through when supporters failed to raise sufficient funds to build an auditorium that would hold four thousand people.

Rotary International held its Seventeenth Annual Convention in Denver on June 14–18, 1926. In the final count, 8,890 Rotarians, many of them shown here in front of the Denver Municipal Auditorium, attended the 1926 convention. Photo courtesy Denver Rotary Club.

Charles Gates, Sr., shown here with his son, Charles, Jr., had been active in Denver Rotary since its earliest years. He is likely one of a handful of Rotarians who pitched in the final $80,000 to finish construction on the Cosmopolitan Hotel before the 1926 Rotary International Convention. Photo courtesy Denver Public Library Western History Department.

Closing the deal for Denver the following year could be credited to Dr. John Andrew from Longmont, who just happened to be a member of the International Convention Committee. At forty-five, the Illinois-born physician had quite an impressive resumé. A University of Colorado alumnus, he founded Longmont Hospital early in his career and later became president of the Colorado Hospital Association. Andrew became governor of the Seventh District of RI in 1924 and a member of the Educational Committee the following year. One of five representatives serving on the 1925–26 Convention Committee, he sold Denver's desirability as a convention destination and summer vacation spot, which *The Rotarian* described as, "a city of 300,000 in the midst of America's Switzerland." Andrew probably had background support from Paul Harris and Chesley Perry, but in any case, he must have been very persuasive.

Once Denver had the convention on the calendar, locals needed to determine exactly how to deal with the twelve to fifteen thousand members and wives who would pour into the city. According to the May 1926 *Rotarian*, conventioneers and spouses had 2,800 hotel rooms and "1,000 rooms in the finest houses in the city" at their disposal. Since Denver lacked sufficient hotel space to accommodate the crowd, a few unnamed Rotarians (possibly led by Charles Gates and H. Brown Cannon) raised $80,000 to complete the Cosmopolitan Hotel. An extension of Frank Edbrooke's 1889 Metropole Hotel at Seventeenth and Broadway, the Cosmo opened June 5, just in time for the convention. The hotel would give way to a parking lot in May 1984 after serving Rotarians as a meeting space for decades.

Although the Denver-based Continental Oil Company (which later became Conoco) urged Rotarians to travel by automobile, promising "improved roads all the way," railroads seduced conventioneers with special summer tourist rates. Interestingly, one could travel round trip to Denver from Vancouver, British Columbia, for $81.40 while the same journey from New York City cost $96.32. The fare from Kansas City, Missouri, came in at $27.85, which translates to approximately $338 today. Since Denver had no real airport until 1929, it's doubtful that many chose to "fly the friendly skies."

The Cosmopolitan Hotel, the new location for club meetings and offices, would be completed just in time for the convention. The hotel would accommodate Denver Rotary offices and activities for nearly six decades. Photo courtesy Denver Public Library Western History Department.

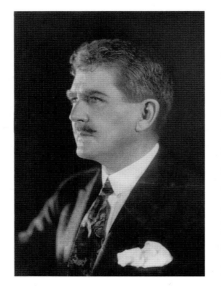

The bombastic Fred Bonfils promoted the 1926 Rotary International Convention in The Denver Post *for months before the event. Photo courtesy Denver Public Library Western History Department.*

Rotarian Fred Bonfils, publisher of *The Denver Post,* got locals on board, rolling out the red carpet and black ink months in advance. (A few members actually resigned when the flamboyant Bonfils joined Rotary and returned when he dropped out.) Along with the Rotary agenda, the *Post* would faithfully cover every detail of the convention, from a mini-Cheyenne Frontier Days rodeo at Overland Park to a Flying Circus and "grand siesta and tea for the ladies at Cheesman Park." [The copy should have read, "fiesta," a misprint that surely cost some editor his job.] Mrs. Charles (Hazel Rhoads) Gates coordinated events for Rotary wives and daughters, including a forum on "Women's Rotary World," featuring speakers from eight nations, and a pageant celebrating "Wildflowers of the Rocky Mountains."

A HOT TIME IN THE OLD TOWN TONIGHT

The convention kicked off June 14 with a gala at the University of Denver Stadium, dubbed by the *Post* "a kaleidoscope vision of the universal and international Rotary tinged with the atmosphere of Western Indian Days." Rotarians had been promised the Old West and Denver duly delivered, with members of the Zuni, Navajo, and Blackfoot Tribes performing tribal dances sprinkled with obligatory war whoops. Other groups greeting international guests included the Black Horse Cavalry from Cheyenne and approximately one thousand marching Highlander Boys (a group formed by Rotarian George Olinger), Boy Scouts, DeMolays, and Denver high school cadets, with music provided by the Denver Municipal Band. In all, nearly two thousand turned out to welcome the international guests. Unfortunately, illness prevented Paul Harris from attending the convention.

The Denver Post, shown here in the 1930s, supported Denver Rotary and enthusiastically publicized the club's activities and charities for decades. Photo courtesy Denver Public Library Western History Department.

The Denver Post rolled out the red carpet for visiting Rotarians. Photo courtesy Denver Rotary Club.

THE TWO ROTARY ANNS

The very active Denver Ladies of Rotary formally organized in 1926–27, just in time for the International Convention. Rotarian wives, known as "Rotary Anns," had been involved with the club for years, helping to organize picnics and other social events. The term apparently originated at the 1915 Rotary International Convention in Houston. Henry J. Brunnier, RI second vice president in 1917–18 and later designer of the San Francisco–Oakland Bay Bridge, told the following story in the November 1951, "By the Way" column in *The Rotarian*:

Rotarians gathered in front of the Cosmo. Note the one lone female in a sea of men. Photo courtesy Rotary International.

"In 1914, the western clubs joined to start a special train from San Francisco to Houston, Tex. for the convention there. Until we got to Los Angeles, my Ann was the only woman on board, so someone gave her the nickname, Rotary Ann."

Since everyone was in a partying mood, he continued, on the way, "all sorts of stunts were planned and someone wrote a Rotary Ann chant. When we arrived in Houston, some Rotarians grabbed Ann, put her on their shoulders and marched around the depot singing this chant. We were all kids then, remember." In Houston, the Brunniers met Guy Gundaker, future RI president in 1923–24, whose wife's name also was Ann. When Gundaker began introducing his wife at conventions as "my Rotary Ann," the name stuck.

After relating the charming tale, the columnist observed that Rotary International frowned on the use of the word *Rotary* in any women's organizations, noting that in 1949–50, the Board ruled that "there shall be no legally recognized women's club auxiliary to Rotary Clubs."

"Sounds pretty final," he pompously observed.

Most activities, including all plenary sessions, took place in the twenty-two-thousand-seat Denver Auditorium. Once the sun went down, visitors were treated to "the greatest electrical display the city has ever given," thanks to Rotarian David Dwight Sturgeon, head of Sturgeon Electric Company and the inventor of outdoor Christmas lighting. Other activities would be held at the Albany Hotel or the House of Friendship across from the Auditorium, formerly the Bon Ton Dance Hall, which offered a comfortable veranda with brightly colored furniture and radio dance music interspersed with convention announcements. The city closed off the entire block

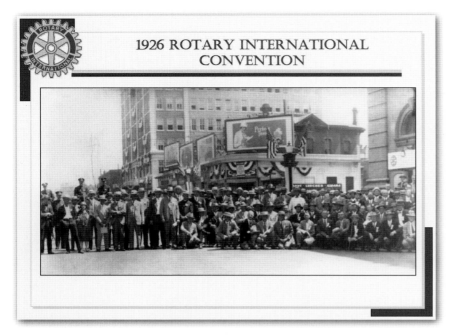

1926 ROTARY INTERNATIONAL CONVENTION

Rotarians celebrated the convention with gusto. Unfortunately, illness prevented founder Paul Harris from attending. Photo courtesy Rotary International.

between Fourteenth and Fifteenth and Champa Streets for the convenience of conventioneers.

Of course, World Peace was high on the agenda. Rotary archives contain a letter to Congress dated June 13, 1926—the day before the convention—supporting the ill-fated Harding Hughes proposal, which promoted United States participation in the Hague World Court. The letter had been signed by prominent Denverites including John Evans (banker and grandson of the former governor), Morrison Shafroth (senatorial/gubernatorial candidate, strong opponent of the Ku Klux Klan in Colorado), Harold Kountze (banker), Louise Iliff (daughter of cattle baron John Wesley Iliff and Elizabeth Iliff Warren), Frances Wayne (*Denver Post* reporter), George Norlin (University of Colorado president), and Henry Toll (lawyer and state legislator). Other matters under discussion included Business Methods, Boys Work, Rotary Education, and Classifications.

Rotarians from around the world attended the 1926 convention, including representatives from South Africa and Japan, 25 from Great Britain and Ireland, 17 from Australia, and 33 from New Zealand, for a total head count of 8,890. To keep the international audience updated on conference happenings, a Rotary sponsored 'round-the-world broadcast emanated from Denver's KOA Radio.

With a motto like "Sunshine and Snowballs Denver '26," visiting Rotarians naturally expected the fluffy white stuff, even in June. After all, if snow in summer

Rotarian David Dwight Sturgeon, arranged for a lighting display at the Denver Auditorium during the convention. Sturgeon invented outdoor Christmas lighting in 1914 to entertain a sick child. Photo courtesy Denver Public Library Western History Department.

could be arranged for the 1908 Democratic National Convention, why not for Rotary International? Sure enough, on June 16, the *Post* published a front-page story on the "Battle of the Nations," a snowball fight between twelve "captivating bathing beauties," and Rotarians from around the world. Naturally, the swimsuit brigade, dance students and performers at the nearby America Theater, won the match.

As the convention wound down and the last conventioneer went home—or, in many cases, off to enjoy a mountain vacation, both *The Rotarian* and *The Denver Post* deemed the event a great success. Denver business considered this a true victory for the West, since the new Rotary International (a name adopted in 1922) president would be Harry H. Rogers of San Antonio, Texas. Upon accepting the honor, President Rogers promised to "put more fellowship and friendship" into Rotary and place special emphasis on business methods, Rotary education, boys work and community service."

Mr. Gero, head gardener at Elitch's, poses next to a flowerbed as Denver welcomed the Rotary International Convention in 1926. Photo courtesy Denver Public Library Western History Department.

DENVER ROTARY AND THE DENVER AND SALT LAKE RAILWAY

The huge snow mound in front of the House of Friendship on Curtis Street reached Denver "direct from the ermine slopes of Corona" in two rail cars, courtesy of the Denver, Northwestern and Pacific Railway (a.k.a. Denver and Salt Lake Railway), an entity Rotary had supported since the club's beginning. Denver Rotary's first treasurer, Harry Beatty, was a vice president of First National Bank, which took over receivership of the Denver, Northwestern and Pacific Railroad, after bank president David Moffat defaulted on several loans. Many Rotarians were likely investors or bank customers. (Moffat, one of Denver's original movers and shakers, died in New York City in 1911 while trying to raise money for the project.) The railroad, subsequently renamed the Denver and Salt Lake Railway, never extended to Salt Lake City. The Denver and Rio Grande absorbed the line in 1947, thus obtaining control of the Moffat Road and the Moffat Tunnel under the Continental Divide.

Although winter travel was nearly impossible until the Tunnel opened in 1928, summer along the line was a thing of beauty, and tourist travel was heavy during the 1920s. Posters advertised daily excursions to the "Top of the World," and on weekends, visitors could travel to the town of Tolland in Boulder Park for $2 and Corona for $3.75.

Visitors explore the long-awaited Moffat Tunnel, which opened to traffic in 1928. Photo courtesy Rosemary Fetter.

OUT-OF-TOWNERS

The Denver club gained status in the Rotary community after 1926, and members subsequently were strongly encouraged to attend international conventions. The following year saw twelve Denver delegates (not counting wives and children) travel to Ostend, Belgium, including former Rotary president Ralph Mayo.

Just six years before Nazi dictator Adolf Hitler took control of Germany, the Belgium convention again stressed the need for a permanent peace in Europe. In an article from *The Rotarian* titled "Ostend Impressions," J. A. E. Verkade, a past president of Rotary International, stated ominously, "We are, in Europe, in a most precarious position. The horrible ordeal we have gone through some years back has sown distrust, ill feeling and even jealousy. . . ." Although Rotarians worldwide promised to do their part in building a peaceful future, farseeing members of the organization could already feel the winds of another war blowing at their backs.

In Denver, club bulletins were casting a wider net, promoting attendance at inter-city meetings, including Boulder, Colorado Springs, and Pueblo. Still, it was a struggle to get Rotarians out of Denver, particularly for meetings in Pueblo, 110 miles and hours away by train. Although the jazzy new Ford Model A could whiz along at 60 m.p.h., the car would need a better road than Highway 85-87, which was still an uneven two-lane path that got bumpier north of Colorado Springs. The Denver committee chair nevertheless complained on September 11, 1928: "This talk about Rotarians being so busy they can't attend an inter-city meeting is all bunk. They waste more time in one week lighting cigars and discussing politics than it takes to attend two inter-city meetings. We ought to have 91 to 100 Rotarians at Pueblo."

As it turned out, Rotary cancelled the upcoming meeting due to candidate Herbert Hoover's appearance in Pueblo that evening. Colorado boosters hoped that Hoover's election would switch the national focus to the West, since he had grown up in Oregon and graduated from Stanford University. Harry Burnham, head of the Denver Tourist Bureau, spoke to Rotarians in April 1929, prophesizing optimistically that Hoover's election "should turn the tide of progress Westward . . .Colorado and Denver will soon occupy the same position to the traveling public that Switzerland does to Europe, both a destination and a gateway." Unfortunately, Hoover would be felled by the Great Depression before he had an opportunity to do much for Colorado tourism.

MATTERS OF INTEREST

Other guest speakers reflected the club's concerns and causes during the Roaring Twenties. Denver Rotary had supported the creation of Rocky Mountain National Park since 1914, when the club appointed naturalist and park advocate Enos A. Mills an honorary Rotarian. That year, Denver Rotary appointed a committee to work with other organizations, Congress, and President Woodrow Wilson to secure a Rocky Mountain National Park out of Estes Park. The Rocky Mountain National Park Act became law on January 26, 1915, but by 1928, Colorado still had not ceded jurisdiction of park roads to the federal government.

IT'S STILL A MYSTERY

Every week the club's newsletter, which became *Mile High Keyway* in 1941, featured a biography about one of the members. In 1929, one legendary entry following Emory Afton's bio stated cryptically, "Birthplace uncertain, as the event occurred during an Indian Uprising."

On January 24, 1929, Denver Rotary scheduled a talk on the history of Rocky Mountain National Park by the park's superintendent Roger Toll. Apparently, a future meeting was being planned to discuss arguments opposing secession of park roads to the federal government. The Denver Rotary Board received a letter of concern in December 1928, signed by a group of Rotarians, including charter member Newcomb Cleveland, and Ralph Broadhurst, who were working for the passage of necessary legislation at the next General Assembly.

"Already the Park has suffered the loss of nearly one-half million dollars which the Government could not appropriate for improvements," the authors complained. "We protest very earnestly against any sympathy on the part of our Club toward a matter which was determined some 15 years ago and by the results of which we must abide." Apparently, Rotary dropped the matter after Toll's presentation and Governor William H. Adams signed the bill ceding jurisdiction in 1929.

During the remainder of the decade, Denver Rotary continued to focus on Boys Work. One beneficiary, the Olinger Highlanders, or Highlander Boys, had been formed in 1916 by mortician George Olinger, one of the first Denver Rotarians. A self-made man, Olinger left school in ninth grade to work in a harness shop and built his business into one of the largest mortuaries in Denver. His Highlander Boys, specifically geared toward youth ages nine to thirteen, originally comprised approximately one hundred boys ages ten and older, who played baseball in the less affluent Highland section of north Denver. Olinger reputedly set aside $.10 out of every dollar he earned to support

Rotarian George Olinger formed the Highlander Boys to help disadvantaged youth. Photo courtesy Denver Public Library Western History Department.

his organization, which was based on a military model although not militaristic in nature. Although Olinger financed the group alone for years, by 1927 the organization had grown to more than twelve thousand members. Olinger subsequently formed the Highlander Boys Foundation and expanded the Highlanders throughout Colorado and Wyoming. Hard-hit by the Depression, the group enjoyed a renaissance during World War II, but eventually disbanded in 1976, suffering from America's Vietnam War era disenchantment with the military.

On May 19, 1929, Harry E. Huffman (Classification: Motion Picture Theaters) gave fellow Rotarians a vocational talk about "What Rotary has to do with the Motion Picture Business." Denver's most successful theater owner and promoter, Huffman began acquiring local movie houses, starting with the Bluebird in 1922. He subsequently developed Denver's largest chain of movie theaters, including the Tabor Grand and the Broadway, which he converted from vaudeville to movies. Huffman became head of the Convention and Visitor's Bureau during the 1930s, remaining deeply involved with Rotary activities and causes. For decades, the club held its annual Orphan's Christmas party at the Orpheum Theater, the Paramount, or the Aladdin Theater on West Colfax.

Rotarian Harry E. Huffman often hosted the Denver Rotary Orphans' Christmas party at the Orpheum Theater, 1537 Welton Street. An effigy labeled "Old Man Depression" hangs from the marquee, and the sign reads "Good Times Are Here." Photo courtesy Denver Public Library Western History Department.

Rotary also suffered personal losses during the twenties. In 1927, the club expressed condolences on the death of his father Albert to Ira Boyd Humphreys, a well-known aviator who established Denver's first commercial airport in 1919. Rotarian Albert Edmund Humphreys, Sr., a highly successful oil baron, had been one of Denver's most generous philanthropists, giving away nearly a million dollars during his lifetime. He established the Humphreys Foundation, one of many supported by Denver Rotary, in 1922 as Colorado's first foundation. Unfortunately, Albert Humphreys became involved with the Teapot Dome Scandal during the notoriously corrupt Harding administration. Many of his friends were subject to a Congressional investigation, and Humphreys himself had been subpoenaed to testify in the bribery trial of Secretary of the Interior Albert B. Fall. A particularly grisly "accident" with a rifle, which many suspected was either suicide or murder, ended his life in May 1927.

His palatial mansion at 770 Pennsylvania Street once featured forty-two rooms, a large downstairs theater (reputed to be haunted), and a ten-car garage with gas pumps and car wash. Rotarian Ira Boyd Humphreys willed the mansion to the Colorado Historical Society in 1976 for a house museum.

The new Denver City and County Building opened in 1932. Photo courtesy Denver Public Library Western History Department.

A NEW CITY HALL

On September 6, 1928, Mayor Ben Stapleton and project architects gave Rotarians a preview of architectural plans for the new City Hall, slated to replace the 1886 granite behemoth at Fourteenth and Larimer Streets near the Market Street Bridge. The old building had a flamboyant history as the site of the infamous 1894 City Hall War between Governor Davis Waite and disgruntled city employees led by notorious con artist Soapy Smith. Although the relic remained standing until the late 1940s, sentimental Denverites kept the massive bell, which still sits in a mini-park on the former site.

Mayor Ben Stapleton digs in at the groundbreaking ceremony for the Denver City and County Building. Photo courtesy Denver Public Library Western History Department.

The Civic Center project had actually begun in 1906 as part of the City Beautiful movement. Mayor Robert Speer commissioned city planner Charles Mulford Robinson to create a blueprint for the governmental axis of downtown Denver, connecting the State Capitol with the old Arapahoe County Courthouse on Court Place. In 1924, city landscape architect/Rotarian S. R. DeBoer created a new plan for the Civic Center that situated the city government building just west of the original center, with a broad open park space between it and the State Capitol. A political football for twenty-five years, the City and County Building finally became a reality through the efforts of Mayor Ben Stapleton, who squirreled away funds to complete construction in 1932 by postponing other projects. The Beaux Arts neoclassical structure, designed by the thirty-nine-member Allied Architects Association of Denver, drew inspiration from Robinson's original recommendations.

GETTING TOGETHER

Club bulletins were always filled with parties, picnics, Ladies Nights, and plenty of social gatherings. After the 1926 Convention, Denver communicated more freely with other Rotarians worldwide. Locally, the Rotary held regular bowling tournaments with other service organizations, including Kiwanis, Lions, Optimists, Civitans, Gyro, and High Twelve. Scores were faithfully recorded in the club newsletter.

In December 1929, for the first time, the Rotary Anns requested to be present for the Christmas Carol Program, which had become an annual event. Rotarian families have been invited to the party ever since.

A surviving program from an Annual Rotary Stag Night, dated April 28, 1927, provides an interesting view of politics during the era, at least from Denver Rotary's point of view. The satirical presentation, titled, the "Vestal Virgins on Parade," begins with *At the Rotary Banquet* by H. L. Mencken. Since the fiery journalist was one of Rotary's outstanding critics, it's unlikely that he was present to recite the piece himself. (A curmudgeon of dynamic proportions, the journalist lambasted everyone from Democrats and Elks to Southerners, Catholics, Presbyterians, and chiropractors. Criticizing what he considered Rotary's "commercial civilization," Mencken also chastised Rotarians for greeting one another by their first names or nicknames: "The first Rotarian was the first man to call John the Baptist, 'Jack,'" he grumbled.)

The four-act skit that completed the program satirized both Rotary and the "liberated" woman of the 1920s. The "Chant of the Vestals," one of many ditties performed during the show, took pot shots at evangelist Aimee Semple McPherson and reformer Judge Ben Lindsey.

Although Judge Lindsey must have been admired by Rotarians for his work as founder of the juvenile court system, he had antagonized Denver's wealthy businessmen for decades. His famous exposé, *The Beast*, co-authored with New York journalist Harvey J. O'Higgins, graphically detailed his struggle with "organized corruption" in the city and helped squelch Speer's reelection campaign in 1912. Despite his international reputation, Lindsey's espousal of companionate marriage, an easily dissolved marital contract for companionship rather than children, enraged many former supporters. A trumped-up disbarment and opposition from groups ranging from the Ku Klux Klan to the Catholic Church finally led him to leave Colorado later in 1929.

The evening ends with a Rotary Drinking Song, from the future "Reunion of Class of '49 of Rotary International University." (The Rotary International University had been proposed in the May 1927 article in *The Rotarian* by Dr. D. E. Phillips, Department of Psychology, the University of Denver.)

Since Prohibition was still in effect until Roosevelt repealed the Eighteenth Amendment in 1933, it's hard to say how much drinking Rotarians actually did, collectively or individually. However, in March 1929 the club put on an "Old Timers" program featuring members from 1911 and 1912. The newsletter advertised, "The [unnamed] members promise to put on one of the meetings of bygone days. With exception of one detail—and there's a law against that."

Presumably, they meant Prohibition.

ROTARY DRINKING SONG
From Stag Night program, circa 1927

We're marching to the altar
Where free love reigns supreme
To try companionate marriage
We hope it's not a dream
We don't know whom we'll find there
We really do not care
This dull life's gone forever
Cause we're out to do or dare
We haven't had a chance, boys
And this is not a bluff
We'll put the skids to Aimeee
When we start to strut OUR stuff

Drink! Drink! Drink! To the old
*   varsity*
Our school of free love and good will
Drink! Drink! Drink!
We are the old grads
Just bums from the Rotary Mill
Drink! Drink! Drink!
We got lots of service for someone to
*   take*
Let's drink.

CITY POLITICS

Although the club rallied behind Mayor Ben Stapleton when he put the finishing touches on Speer's City Beautiful, even city boosters balked at the new airport, which opened in October 1929, just a few days before the Stock Market Crash. Suspicious critics were quick to point out that Rotarian Stapleton had purchased the dairy farm on which he built the airport from another high profile Rotarian, H. Brown Cannon. According to historian Tom Noel, "The airport cost the city $143,013 for the 640-acre site and another $287,000 for four gravel runways, one hangar, a tiny terminal, and a wind sock." Dubbed "Stapleton's Folly" and "Snake Hollow" by opponents, the airport, like Denver International Airport sixty years later, would be criticized for excessive costs and a remote location on the outskirts of the city. Partly as a result, city auditor George Begole edged Stapleton out in the 1932 mayoral race. Naturally, an immediate recall petition emerged, which the Election Commission invalidated because 1) more than half the signatures were bogus and 2) the recall was illegally managed by an election commissioner under a false name.

On January 3, 1935, during the height of the Depression, Begole gave a Rotary presentation on "What's Ahead for 1935." Known for his stand against wasteful

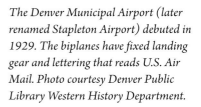

The Denver Municipal Airport (later renamed Stapleton Airport) debuted in 1929. The biplanes have fixed landing gear and lettering that reads U.S. Air Mail. Photo courtesy Denver Public Library Western History Department.

High-ranking Rotarian H. Brown Cannon stands in front of his business, Windsor Dairy. Cannon came under fire when Mayor Ben Stapleton, a fellow Rotarian, purchased his dairy farm and surrounding property to build Stapleton Airport. Photo courtesy Denver Public Library Western History Department.

Mayor George Begole, an active Rotarian, fought a losing battle for a more efficient government. Photo courtesy Denver Public Library Western History Department.

government spending and poor economic practices (he once absconded with a police car when officers left it parked with the engine running), he reported that the city budget was down 25 percent. The Observer, who must have been a Stapleton fan, wrote that, "Denver is going to be the most moral and best governed city in the world if George has anything to say about it. The Observer assumes that George will continue to keep Denver free from snakes; the Rotary Club expects and demands it. And we'll build him a St. Patrick memorial statue."

Both Begole and Stapleton apparently belonged to the club at the same time, although Stapleton dropped out after the election and returned in August 1935. At one meeting, at a table hosted by Begole, they were actually seated together, which must have been interesting. Stapleton took office again in 1936 and, with the help of federal government, continued his program of civic improvements, including Red Rocks Park and Amphitheater. An earlier milestone, and a longtime Rotary goal, had been the February 26, 1928 opening of the 6.21-mile Moffat Tunnel under the Continental Divide. The tunnel's pioneer bore became a vital aqueduct for thirsty Denver, diverting water from the Fraser River on the Western Slope through the tunnel and providing a water supply for the developing suburbs.

ROTARY CODE OF ETHICS

In 1932, Rotarian Herbert J. Taylor created The Four-Way Test, a code of ethics adopted by Rotary eleven years later. The test, which has been translated into more than one hundred languages, asks:

Of the things we think, say or do
Is it the TRUTH?
Is it FAIR to all concerned?
Will it build GOODWILL and BETTER FRIENDSHIPS?
Will it be BENEFICIAL to all concerned?

HARD TIMES

The Stock Market Crash of October 29, 1929, had been slow to affect Denver, but by late 1930, nearly every club bulletin made some reference to the difficult economy. On November 9, 1930, Rotarian Windfield Hartzell (who dropped out of Denver Rotary the following year) distributed the following statement to the club: "There surely must be something wrong with a system that makes it possible for 5,000,000 to drop out of work and 10,000,000 to be working only part time." The statement called for emergence of new leadership, and on November 25, a letter from Club President W. F. R. Mills urged Rotarians to exert "every effort possible to stimulate employment." Mills encouraged each member to keep all employees possible on the payroll, "and if any improvements were contemplated at the home or place of business, that such improvements be done now."

Still, the newsletter sadly published names of departing members who had either lost their businesses or left the club for unstated reasons. By 1933, the worst year of the Depression, one in four adults was out of work. Rotary expenditures exceeded income that year, resulting in a shortfall of $600.68. New members continued to join, however, and Rotarians managed to keep up their spirits despite the gloom. Ladies Nights, Fathers and Sons and Fathers and Daughters celebrations and picnics at Elitch's continued as usual,

The Opportunity School at Thirteenth and Welton Streets had its own auto shop. Rotarians were great supporters of Emily Griffith, who spoke at the club on several occasions. Photo courtesy Denver Public Library Western History Department.

although the newsletter contained fewer jokes. On July 9, 1931, the club introduced a new streamlined version of the luncheon program/newsletter, which "we have tried to make attractive and compact and we sincerely hope you like it."

The philanthropic focus during the decade continued to be Boys Work. On September 3, 1931, the Boys Work Committee reported expenditures for 1928–29 at $4,781.50, and for 1929–30 at $6,486.40. In 1930–31, the club's financial support kept eighty boys in high school.

On March 3, 1932, members welcomed back speaker Emily Griffith, principal of Denver Opportunity School. Denver Rotarians had been strong supporters of Griffith's work since 1916, when the Denver Public Schools converted Longfellow School at Fourteenth and Welton Streets into Opportunity School. Thanks to Griffith, Denver became the first city in the world to offer free universal adult education. Countless immigrants and even natives learned to read, write, and speak proper English, and in the process had been trained with marketable job skills. Despite her protest, the school was renamed Emily Griffith Opportunity School when she retired in 1933, a year after her Rotary talk.

Although many early membership rosters are missing from Denver Rotary Archives, the listings for 1931–34 include businesses that lasted for decades, along with the names of prominent locals such as L. C. McClure, Photographer; M. W. Gano, Jr.,

Club 31 celebrated its Twenty-fifth Anniversary on December 1, 1936. Several of the club's first members were still around to celebrate. Photo courtesy Denver Rotary Club.

Denver Rotary President William E. Russell stands on the speaker's right during a Rotary celebration circa 1938–39. Photo courtesy the Knight family.

Retail Clothing (Gano-Downs); A. Bowman, Cracker and Biscuit Manufacturer; Fred Davis, President of Davis Furniture Company; S. R. DeBoer, Landscape Architect; J. P. Jonas, Jonas Brothers Furs; James "Quigg" Newton, Boettcher, Newton and Company; Henry Everett Sachs, Sachs-Lawlor; Robert C. Van Schaak, Building Management; and Charles E. Wells, Wells Music Company.

THE NEW DEAL

As the economy continued to decline, even the club's Republicans were relieved when fellow Rotarian Franklin D. Roosevelt won the presidency in 1932. A member of the Rotary Club of Albany, Roosevelt was quoted in a district conference speech, when he called the organization "a powerful and stabilizing factor" in world relations. The following year, on March 9, the club bulletin optimistically reported, "For a generation Rotary has been stressing the ideal of service as a business keynote, and now the president of the United States [in his inaugural] has definitely given consideration to this principle."

By January 15, 1935, longtime Rotarian Charles C. Gates was telling the club that "business is certainly better right now and constantly improving under the New Deal." Not everyone agreed with all of Roosevelt's ideas, however. Roy Sampson (Classification: Law-Mining) reported to the club on the Social Security Act and all its ramifications, to the confusion of many members. The Observer remarked, "I for one agree with Roy—it's a mess."

THE ROTARY WHEEL

The longest line of Denver Rotarians still active in the club began with Fred White, who joined in 1933 (Classification Machine Shop). In 2010, his grandson, Jim White, recalled his family involvement in Rotary over the decades. "I recently found the pattern my grandfather used to make bronze bookends with the Rotary seal," he said. "Grandfather would give them to club presidents and members all over the world."

The May 26, 1932 newsletter contains a reference to a large Rotary wheel, which was displayed in the meeting room for the first time. "This wheel has six spokes and 24 teeth," the newsletter noted. "From time to time, the membership has suggested that the wheel of the club is symbolic of the activities of the club and its members." A gear wheel represented service, with the cogs as members, each having a part in the organization's work and interacting with one another. The cogs were held together by the rim, which signified the club. The spokes were the club meetings, while the drive of the central shaft symbolized Rotary International.

Rotarian Scott White holds the bronze bookends with the Rotary seal that his great-grandfather, Fred White, presented to visiting club presidents and members all over the world. Photo courtesy Jim White.

On December 1, Rotary celebrated its Twenty-fifth Anniversary at the Silver Glade Room of the Cosmopolitan Hotel, attended by charter members and past district governors including John Andrew, George Olinger and J. Claire Evans. Harry Barrett, past president in 1916-1917, told Rotarians "How History Was Made," although details were not related in the newsletter/program. Guest tickets for the men's meeting were $1.50, with business attire required.

By 1938, Rotary guest speakers included a young Quigg Newton, Jr. (future Denver mayor), who detailed fair trade practices, and John R. Hermann, commanding officer of the Colorado-Wyoming Civilian Conservation Corps, who spoke on the constructive work of the CCC. "A visit to our Mountain Parks and elsewhere in the state confirms his story," said the Observer.

On August 31, 1939, the Annual Picnic at Elitch's would be tainted by the news of Hitler's invasion of Poland and the beginning of World War II. The evils of Nazi Germany would put RI's policy of political neutrality to the toughest test ever, causing many Rotarians, including Paul Harris, to shift to the other side in the name of humanity.

No one could have foreseen the far-reaching consequences of the next five years. By the end of the War, Rotarians would be living in a new America—and a new Denver.

Gayle Wootten Jenkins, mother of Denver Rotarian Rike Wootten, married Ray Jenkins in January 1940. In this photo, they are celebrating their honeymoon at the Rotary International Convention in Hawaii, June 21, 1940. Photo courtesy Rike Wootten.

It's the friendly smile and the kindly hand-shake at a Rotary Convention that is always remembered longer than the most spectacular entertainment feature.

—*Mile High Keyway*, June 12, 1941

Attractive young women pose atop the roof of the Brown Palace Hotel, circa 1940s, with an equally impressive view of Denver in the background. Photo courtesy Denver Public Library Western History Department.

CHAPTER III

World War II and the Postwar Era
1941–1951

DENVER'S SECOND
ROTARY INTERNATIONAL CONVENTION

Although Rotary International had originally scheduled the 1941 Convention in Toronto, Canada, in January *The Rotarian* announced that the Canadian government had taken over the exposition grounds, ostensibly for military purposes. The Selection Committee subsequently accepted an offer from Denver, which joined with forty-five other Colorado Rotary Clubs to host the city's second International Convention. Toronto would be rescheduled for the 1942 Convention.

This photo of Sixteenth Street, circa 1940, shows Lerner Shops, Joslins Dry Goods Store, and the Tabor Movie Theater. Photo courtesy Denver Public Library Western History Department.

Governor Ralph Carr (right) presents a ten-gallon hat to RI President Armondo de Arruda Pereira at the RI Convention as Bernice Head, Walter Head, Toni Pereira, and a group of Native Americans look on. Photo courtesy Rotary International.

As convention preparations were made, the newsletter reminded Rotarians that official regalia included the ten-gallon hat, "available at D&F for $1.30." The week before the convention, an International Assembly at the Broadmoor hosted a gathering of district governors and officers to discuss activities for the coming year.

On June 14, after the meeting, the group planned to dedicate a bronze and stone Rotary Monument atop Mount Evans, but bad weather made the road impassable. New RI President Tom J. Davis of Butte, Montana, presided over the rescheduled ceremony on August 15, attended by several members including the elderly but still active W. F. R. Mills, former president of Denver Rotary. Rotarians sealed a copper case containing club records, books, photographs, and other materials in a stone crypt behind the bronze door. The time capsule, still atop Mount Evans, will be opened in 2041.

The plaque read: *Presented by the members of Rotary Clubs in the 113th district, Rotary International, dedicated to the service and pleasure of all mankind. Unveiled by Armando de Arruda Pereira, Sao Paulo, president Rotary International, 32nd Annual Convention, Denver, Colorado, June 1941.*

On June 15, Denver welcomed nearly ten thousand enthusiastic Rotarians, becoming only the fifth city in history to host a Rotary International convention for a second time.

On August 15, 1941, local NBC affiliate station KOA Radio broadcast the speech as RI President Tom Davis addressed the Denver Rotary Club. Photo courtesy Rotary International.

Although attendance from outside North America had diminished due to the war, thirty countries, including England, would be represented.

The convention opened with a rousing welcome by RI President Armando de Arruda Pereira, Denver Rotary President L. Ward Bannister, and Denver Mayor Ben Stapleton, who had arranged for completion of the Denver Auditorium annex just in time to accommodate the large crowd. Another civic project, Red Rocks Park and Amphitheater, also got a jump-start because of the convention. The theater's June 16 dedication, attended by more than nine thousand Rotarians, was a spectacular event and a coup for both Denver Rotary and the Stapleton administration.

Rotary pioneer Chesley A. Perry, who spoke at the 1941 Convention, provided invaluable assistance during the formation of Denver Rotary thirty years earlier. Photo courtesy Rotary International.

Atop Mount Evans, RI President Tom Davis places a copper case containing club materials in a stone crypt for a time capsule to be opened in 2041. Standing directly behind Davis are (left to right) L. Ward Bannister, P. Hicks Cadle, W. F. R. Mills, and Ralph B. Mayo. Photo courtesy Denver Rotary Club.

On June 15, 1941, the city welcomed nearly ten thousand enthusiastic Rotarians at the newly completed Red Rocks Amphitheater. Denver became only the fifth city in history to host the Rotary International Convention for a second time. Photo courtesy Denver Rotary Club.

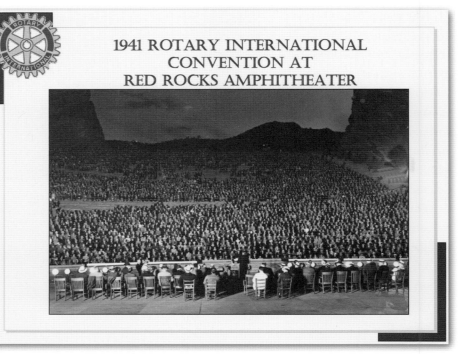

1941 ROTARY INTERNATIONAL CONVENTION AT RED ROCKS AMPHITHEATER

Rotary founder Paul P. Harris advocated abandonment of the traditional policy of neutrality. He declared, "We do not want lunatics or despots as neighbors, whether in Europe or elsewhere. . . ." Photo courtesy Rotary International.

Despite Australia's 1939 entry into World War II, Samuel J. Janes of Sydney, Angus Mitchell of Melbourne, and Stanley Perry of Perth made it to the 1941 Convention. Australia would play a key role in the War in the Pacific from 1942 to 1944. Photo courtesy Rotary International.

Rotarians held major convention events at the Denver Auditorium. Photo courtesy Rotary International.

The conference theme quickly became *The Rotarian Amid World Conflict*, and in unprecedented addresses, three speakers, including Rotary founder Paul P. Harris advocated abandonment of the group's traditional position of neutrality. Harris de-

clared, "We do not want lunatics or despots as neighbors, whether in Europe or elsewhere . . . as sure as the fact that Europe arose from the devastation of the mad men of former days, it will arise again. The morning will come. The great question is, shall we be prepared to face its momentous challenges?" Harris also urged Rotarians to continue international programs and work toward a new, more effective League of Nations after the war.

While the men held plenary sessions and gave speeches, their wives and daughters attended parties and a fashion show. On June 17, Marjorie (Mrs. Temple) Buell, assisted by Florence (Mrs. Harry C.) Brown, wife of the host executive committee chairman, threw an outdoor fiesta and tea for the ladies at the 160-acre Buell estate on South University Boulevard. Costumed actors in western garb greeted guests and the lawn was dotted with tintype booths and other concessions. Meanwhile, according to the *Rocky Mountain News*, daughters of Rotary members "wandered the grounds with baskets of flowers and cherries."

Denver Rotarian Ben Mark Cherrington (left) receives a Certificate of Appreciation at the 1941 Convention for his work in International Affairs. Cherrington would become an author of the Charter of the United Nations, and a cofounder of the United Nations Educational Scientific and Cultural Organization (UNESCO). He was honored by Queen Elizabeth II in 1956 for his contributions to international affairs. Photo courtesy Rotary International.

Rotarian wives Jean Harris (left) and Toni Pereira pose in front of a fountain at City Park. During the 1941 RI Convention, women were entertained by a fashion show, several parties, and an outdoor fiesta and tea at the Buell estate. Photo courtesy Rotary International.

Sergeant-at-arms Richard Wells wields a shillelagh over two unidentified men at the convention. Photo courtesy Rotary International.

Buell's daughter Callae Gilman, who later became a Denver Rotarian, recalled, "We lived in a very large Colonial house which sat about half a block from the street, so it was perfect for the party. We were all dressed in antebellum outfits, as in *Gone with the Wind*. People came by cars and busloads, but they had problems parking between the rows of hay. We were really out in the country then, with farms and alfalfa fields, cows and turkeys, and stables for horses nearby."

Another event for the women, a fashion show at Elitch Gardens, featured original costumes from the movies, loaned by Hollywood film stars. The men joined their wives for district dinners, followed by the President's Ball at the Denver Auditorium and a barbecue at Lakeside Amusement Park as a grand finale. Naturally, the ubiquitous Harry Huffman organized the entertainment.

Rotarians enjoy a levitation act during a meeting. Hopefully, the subject made it back to earth without incident. Photo courtesy of the Knight family.

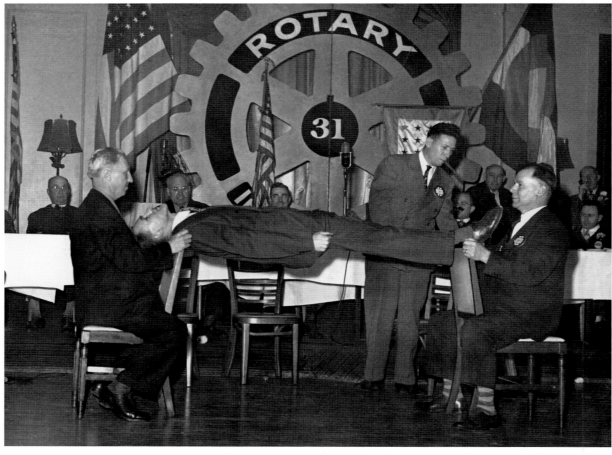

DEDICATION OF RED ROCKS AMPHITHEATER AND PARK

When Red Rocks Amphitheater officially opened (to echoing Rotary applause), the entertainment venue fulfilled its promise as a spectacular addition to Denver's Mountain Parks System. At the turn of the twentieth century, John Brisben Walker, Sr., amusement park entrepreneur and *Cosmopolitan* magazine founder, had been the first to recognize Red Rocks' potential. Walker called the area "the Garden of the Titans" and built an observation deck, funicular railway, and roadway to a primitive theater, where he held concerts beginning in 1910. By the time Denver purchased the

With the assistance of the Civilian Conservation Corps, George Cranmer, manager of Parks and Improvements, rushed to complete the Red Rocks Amphitheater in time for the RI Convention. Photo courtesy Denver Public Library Western History Department.

land from Walker in 1928, the deck and railway were long gone, but for $50,000, Red Rocks still was quite a bargain. Although Mayor Stapleton preferred to leave the area in its natural state, George Cranmer, manager of parks and improvements, wanted to build a classical outdoor theater like one he had seen at Taorima in Sicily. Although money was scarce in the 1930s, Stapleton and Cranmer managed to obtain funds from the Work Projects Association and laborers from the Civilian Conservation Corps. Anticipating Stapleton's objection to a more expensive project than anticipated, Cranmer picked a day when the mayor was out of town to clear the ground between two large boulders to make room for seating. The CCC dynamited with one huge blast and the giant rock garden was no more. Faced with a *fait accompli*, Stapleton allowed Cranmer to hire architect Burnham Hoyt, who designed the theater and seating.

The spectacular opening received national coverage on CBS and a spread in *TIME* magazine. Entertainment, according to the *Rocky Mountain News*, included a performance by the Ogallala Sioux from Pine Ridge, South Dakota (apparently there weren't enough Native Americans left in Colorado), the Nordic Ensemble from Duluth, Minnesota, and the Denver Municipal Chorus. Metropolitan Opera star Helen Jepson, a lyric soprano famous for both her voice and her stunning blonde beauty, won the night with a performance of "Ah, fos e lui" from Verdi's Opera, *La Traviata*. She later maintained, "This theater sings for you."

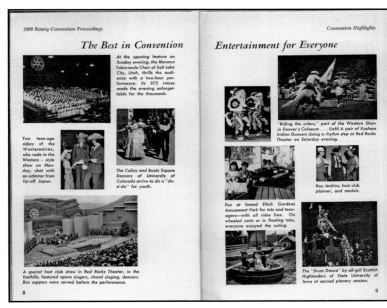

Highlights of the 1941 RI Convention included a concert at Red Rocks. Photo courtesy Denver Rotary Club.

THE WAR ERA

The tumultuous international situation remained on everyone's mind long after the last conventioneer had gone home. Denver Rotary joined other local organizations to collect items like razor blades for British soldiers and appointed representatives to participate in the Rotary International National Service Committee, which entertained soldiers in military camps. That summer, Rotarians requested one hundred cars and drivers from the membership to take soldiers from Lowry Field on a 3.5-hour mountain trip to Genesee and Central City.

Lowry would become an important feature in the Denver landscape during the next few decades. As early as 1937, the city persuaded the Army to "go West" by donating the old Agnes Phipps Memorial Sanitarium at East Sixth Avenue and Quebec Street, along with an additional 960 acres, to build the Army Air Corps Technical School. On February 26, 1938, the school became Lowry Field, formally dedicated in honor of Second Lieutenant Francis B. Lowry, a pilot killed in France during World War I and buried in adjacent Fairmount Cemetery. During the war, Lowry would be expanded and Buckley Field added to the Denver military scene.

The Japanese attack on Pearl Harbor on December 7, 1941, plunged the United States into the Second World War. Rotarian Charles C. Gates and his wife, Hazel, who owned a home in Honolulu, experienced the attack firsthand. Hazel Gates shared the details at the March 5, 1942 Rotary meeting, warning against indifference to danger even in Denver, where a mid-continent location seemed fairly safe in the days before ICBM missiles and the atom bomb.

"She [Mrs. Gates] brings a simple, clear and yet dramatic story to us all with the punch of a bomb falling upon our loved ones," wrote the Observer. For the remainder of the war, the letters V . . . -V . . . -V (for Victory) would mark every newsletter.

Due to Denver's remoteness from anything resembling "the action," isolationist sentiments ran high before the attack. However, after December 7 Denverites got on the bandwagon like everyone else in the country, although it took awhile for reality to sink in. On the first Christmas after Pearl Harbor, regardless of blackouts on the coasts, Denver defiantly beamed with bright colored lights that could be seen for miles. *Mile High Keyway* first mentions the U.S. entry into World War II on December 18, urging readers to envision a future Christmas when "the whole world may again rejoice in peace."

As more Rotarians took up arms, the organization added Military Service to the Honorary Memberships, which kept classifications open until after the fighting ended. *Keyway* listed thirty-six sons (and stepsons) of Rotarians in military service on October 8, 1942, a list that would swell during the next three years.

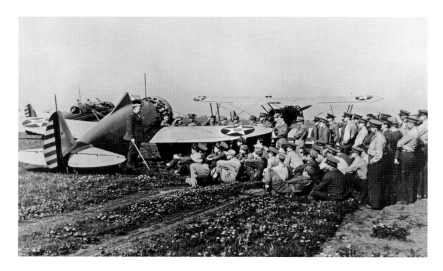

A group of soldiers study airplane nomenclature at Lowry Field. Photo courtesy Tom Noel.

Shortages of meat, dairy, and flour made luncheons a challenge during the war years, as *Keyway* often noted. On July 15, 1943, a report from "The Seeing Eye," as the mysterious Observer was sometimes called, advised members, "For the benefit of you absent members, you missed a few good points last Thursday. We had ham . . . you know, the stuff you used to eat with eggs. Or do you remember eggs?"

In August, Rotarians welcomed the crew of the *Memphis Belle*, nickname of a B-17F Flying Fortress famous for its bombings of German munitions plants. Members were urged to buy more war bonds and participate locally in the war effort. That year, Rotary publications listed twenty countries in which the organization had been disbanded, including Austria, Belgium, Bulgaria, Estonia, Germany, Greece, Hungary, Spain, Japan, and The Netherlands.

Denver's war industries contributed substantially to a booming economy. To the northeast, Rocky Mountain Arsenal, established in 1942, created the lethal gases and napalm bombs used to bring the enemy to its knees. On the site of the seven-thousand-acre Hayden Ranch in Lakewood, Remington's Denver Ordnance Plant (later converted to the Federal Center) made ammunition and produced K-rations for the military. Near Municipal (Stapleton) Airport, Continental Airlines workers reconfigured B-17 and B-29 bombers for wartime duty.

An increased demand for goods also benefited the local economy. The sugar beet industry, which the government discouraged before the war in favor of Hawaii and Cuba, resumed production. Gates Rubber Company prospered until the Japanese captured Singapore and the Dutch Indies, reducing America's rubber to a six-month supply of stockpiled material. Massive rubber drives took place across the country, with people donating their tires, boots, and raincoats to the effort. The Gates Company joined forces with other businesses to form the Copolymer Corporation, which manufactured synthetic rubber and experimented with new materials like nylon and rayon. Between 1941 and 1945, annual production of synthetic rubber in the United States increased from 231 tons to 840,000 tons.

The war also brought about social change. In September 1943, a symposium published in *The Rotarian* examined the question, "Should Women be Paid Equal Wages for Equal Work?" Although opinions varied, P. Hicks Cadle, Denver meat-seasoning manufacturer and future club president, did Denver Rotary proud by stating, "Women are filling men's jobs around the world . . . their paychecks should attest to that fact."

Despite the onset of World War II, Denver lit up for the holidays. Photo courtesy Denver Public Library Western History Department.

A mariachi group serenades Rotarians during a luncheon. Photo courtesy the Knight family.

BOYS WORK DURING WORLD WAR II

If nothing else, the war definitely solved Denver's unemployment issues. High school boys had no problem finding a job after graduation—young men fit for duty already had their work cut out for them. The Rotary's Boys Work Committee, which formed in 1923, continued to provide scholarships for boys in senior high school, beginning in the second term of tenth grade. To apply, a boy needed a B average and the ability to demonstrate economic need. Upon recommendation from a school principal or advisor, his application would be passed on to a member of the Boys Work Committee, who would make a home visit and report on the family's condition. Funds to support the program, approximately $7,000 to $10,000 a year, were raised by voluntary contributions and the club treasury, which provided $500 to $2,000. Students in tenth grade received a monthly check of $7.50 ($91.92 equivalent in 2009); eleventh graders received $10 ($121.90); and twelfth graders, $12.50 ($152.37).

To help younger boys whose fathers might be absent due to the war, in 1944 Rotary took over sponsorship of Boy Scout Troop 201 at Wyman Elementary School, providing items such as flags, banners, and regulation neckties "in Rotary blue and gold." During World War II, Boy Scouts were invaluable to the Office of War Administration and Office of Civilian Defense, distributing posters and even serving as air raid wardens appointed by Denver's Civilian Defense Board.

GOD BLESS ROTARIANS

On February 10, 1991, Denver Rotary received a letter, along with a check for $1,000, from Ralph D. Potter, a retired police division chief. Potter wrote:

"Just before the Great Depression, my father died leaving my mother, a younger sister and me with nothing but the debt of the funeral costs. Jobs were hard to find for educated and qualified men, so it was especially difficult for me and my unskilled mother. I got a job cleaning at a school before and after classes and my mother found similar employment, but our little family, like many others, was barely surviving. Then one day I was called to the school office and handed a five-dollar bill, a gift of the Rotary Club. Five dollars doesn't seem like much, but in the '30s it could provide food for our family for a week.

"In the ensuing months and years I continued to receive these gifts until they totaled $55. When I graduated from high school, I resolved to pay this money some day. I am now in my 70s, a retired police division chief. My two sons are graduates of Yale and Lafayette Universities, pursuing successful engineering careers and my oldest grandson is an engineer with the Houston space program. I can never fully repay the Rotary Club for those gifts so many years ago, they had too great an impact to my life and the lives of my family, but I can and will make a token donation to your organization. God Bless Rotarians."

CLUB MEMBERS STAY UP TO DATE WITH *MILE HIGH KEYWAY*

From the 1920s until the 1950s, the *Mile High Keyway* format remained pretty much the same, an 8.5 by 11 sheet of plain or glossy paper, folded in half, with a scenic photo of Colorado on the cover along with the date and location of the meeting, usually the Silver Glade at the Cosmopolitan, the Lincoln Room of the Shirley Savoy or the Albany Hotel. The name *Mile High Keyway* first appeared on April 20, 1941.

The program would provide a brief introduction to the luncheon speaker, who was generally someone nationally or locally prominent, from Secretary of the Navy James V. Forrestal to Judge J. Edgar Chenoweth of Trinidad and even Richard M. Nixon, Congressional representative from Southern California. Inside, the newsletter/program provided an informal review of the previous week's meeting, with club news on the opposing page. Comments by the anonymous Observer, a position appointed by the president, followed a tradition that dated back to the 1930s. Birthdays, district meetings, international conventions, members visiting other clubs, roster corrections, new members, and Ladies Night or Stag Night information would be noted, along with perfect attendance data. A new military membership might be mentioned during World War II, but oddly, no casualties were listed other than the first son lost to the war, First Lieutenant Alvin Rosenbaum, son of Rotarian Harry Rosenbaum, proprietor of the Western Leather Art Company, Art Goods Manufacturer.

MOVE RI HEADQUARTERS TO DENVER?

In 1944, Rotary International began to seriously consider a move from temporary quarters in the Chicago's Pure Oil Building, opening up selection to all thirty-five hundred cities with Rotary Clubs. Daniels and Fisher Company President A. B. Trot headed a successful campaign that put Denver in the top spot above thirty-seven other competing cities.

It was the beginning of a battle that raged for the next two years.

On February 22, the *Rocky Mountain News* reported that, "Denver Rotary club members have drawn up plans for a $600,000, 'Temple of Rotary' to be built in the old Calvary Cemetery grounds. The building, constructed in classical style, would overlook Cheesman Park and have an unobstructed view of the Rockies."

The *News* further reported that a Rotary International Convention had been tentatively scheduled in May, during which time the proposal would be discussed. The article stated that the Building Committee "lavished praise on Denver," citing the city's healthful climate, scenic beauty, central location, high character of the population and the adequate hotel accommodations "in normal times." The Building Committee was likely swayed by a color film narrated by journalist and Colorado native Lowell Thomas, *The Land of Your Dreams*, which would be shown to Rotary Clubs around the country.

Naturally, Chicago fought back, forming the All-Chicago Executive Committee for the Retention of RI Headquarters. Their brochure questioned, "Shall the great oak called ROTARY International be uprooted from its native

This architectural rendering by Temple Buell shows prospective Rotary International offices in Denver. Dubbed "the Temple of Rotary," the project lacked sufficient backing and Rotary headquarters stayed in Chicago. Photo courtesy Denver Public Library Western History Department.

NOTABLE ROTARIANS OF THE 1940S

TEMPLE HOYNE BUELL

(Joined 1938. Classification: Architecture)

The city's premiere architect, raconteur and man-about-town, Temple (Sandy) Buell was born into a prestigious Chicago family. He moved to Denver in 1921,

Architect Temple Buell is still remembered by many Rotarians for his wit, generosity, and talent. Photo courtesy Tom Noel.

after a wartime bout with poison gas combined with tuberculosis posed serious danger to his health. By 1940, the handsome, 6'4" Buell owned the largest architectural firm in the region. His projects included the Paramount Theater, the original Cherry Creek Shopping Center (he has been called the father of the urban shopping mall), twenty-six area schools, and several government office buildings. Buell also served as city planner for Arapahoe County and helped to design the City of Cherry Hills.

In 1945, Buell created a blueprint for possible Rotary International headquarters in Denver. Although he won rave reviews for his classical design, Rotarians ultimately voted down a move from Chicago to Denver. Buell died in 1990, at age ninety-four, but his dynamic personality, humor, wit, and graciousness as a host are still remembered by Rotarians today. A dedicated philanthropist, he endowed the first Rotary International Scholarship with a $150,000 gift and provided the last $50,000 to put Club 31 fundraising for Polio Plus over the top. His Temple Buell Foundation continues to provide support for programs and initiatives for children, especially in the areas of "early intervention, prevention, and improving the social and educational systems critical to the well-being of Colorado's youngest citizens."

DR. EDGAR "WALLIE" WAHLBURG

(Joined 1942. Classification: Social Centers-Community)

In 1944, *Mile High Keyway* announced that Denver Rotary's own "Wallie" Wahlburg had been named Public Welfare Supervisor for United Nations Relief and Rehabilitation Administration (UNRRA), one of the greatest humanitarian projects in history. Born to the parents of Swedish immigrants, Wahlberg worked his way through the University of Denver's Iliff School of Theology, subsequently taking on the faltering Grace Methodist Church, the urban parish once attended by Denver Rotary founder Gratton Hancock. Transforming Grace into one of the most successful, accepting, and reform-minded churches in Colorado, he ministered to the poor during the 1930s, operating an employment agency, shoe shop, barbershop, and food, clothing, and fuel distribution center through the church. He served the UNRRA in Palestine, Greece, and China through 1946, and has been called an American hero of the Greek Civil War. Wahlburg moved to Dearborn, Michigan, in 1947 to become pastor of the liberal Mount Olivet United Methodist Church and subsequently worked for the War on Poverty. He died in Estes Park in 1991.

ROGER D. KNIGHT, JR.
(Joined 1937. Classification: Bread Baking, Wholesale)

Roger (Bud) Knight, Jr., served as Denver Rotary president in 1944 and spent a great deal of time in service to the club. Knight was the grandson of Denver pioneer Stephen Knight, a major stockholder in J. K. Mullen's Colorado Milling and Elevator Company and an early Denver Rotarian. Observer jokes about his poetry ("The Budding Knight—like his bread—is a half baked poet.") may have led Knight to leave his position as head of Campbell-Sell Baking Company and become president of Denver U.S. National Bank. At a time when Colorado law did not allow branch banking, he and his colleagues made it the strongest bank in the state, ultimately forging the enterprise into United Banks of Colorado.

Rotarians respected Roger (Bud) Knight, Jr., for his integrity and personal warmth. Knight served as Denver Rotary Club president from 1944 to 1945 and remained active in the club all his life. Photo courtesy of the Knight family.

According to his *Rocky Mountain News* obituary in 2007, Knight was a hands-on kind of manager. A former employee, Wells Fargo Regional President David Bailey, recalled the era when Denver-U.S. National Bank had one of the largest drive-through banks in the country. On Friday afternoons, when cars got snarled in traffic at the bank's drive-though maze, Knight would go out in the street in his business suit and direct traffic. On other occasions, "he would go around picking up paper clips because he was afraid someone would slip."

Mount Calvary Cemetery, seen here in the early 1900s, was the projected site for RI Headquarters. Denver Botanic Gardens currently occupies the site. Photo courtesy Denver Rotary.

Chicago and trucked away from the fruitful soil whence its branches spread to the far corners of the earth? UNTHINKABLE!"

On January 9, 1946, C. Paul Harrington of Rotary International delivered a check for $5,000 and the necessary option papers to Archbishop Urban J. Vehr for 18.8 acres on the site of the abandoned Mount Calvary Cemetery on York Street, between Ninth and Eleventh Avenues. If Rotary purchased the land, it would necessitate disinterment of approximately sixty-six hundred bodies, which would be relocated to Mount Olivet Cemetery in Jefferson County. Fortunately, the church had kept records marking the location of each individual, precluding a public spectacle like the disaster that occurred in 1893. That unceremonious removal of corpses from neighboring Mount Prospect Cemetery, the city's first graveyard (now Cheesman Park), inspired ghost stories about the area that persist today.

As it turned out, the convention would be postponed until 1946 and held in Atlantic City, New Jersey, instead. On June 6, members defeated the proposal to move RI to Denver by a vote of 1,815 to 1,359, possibly due to the influence of retired secretary Chesley R. Perry and founder Paul Harris, both of whom preferred that headquarters remain in Chicago. Paul Harris passed away the following year.

Harry Huffman, the eternal city booster, publicly announced that Denver Rotarians would continue the drive and reopen the question at the 1947 San Francisco Convention. Despite Denver's admirable politicking, the proposal was defeated a second time. Although the *Post*, a.k.a. Palmer Hoyt, lauded the work of Denver Rotary President Donald D. Keim, President-elect Lloyd E. Yoder and former President C. Paul Harrington, the paper attributed the failure to "powerful club and business interests," maintaining that "the Denverites were outnumbered but not outfought." In 1958, the Mount Calvary Cemetery land would be converted into the Denver Botanic Gardens.

ROTARY CREATES DENVER BOYS, INC.

In the aftermath of World War II, when many boys were left without fathers, Denver Rotary again put the motto, "Service Above Self," into action. On February 6, 1946, *Mile High Keyway* announced the formation of Denver Boys, Inc. (DBI), whose purpose was "to help boys live healthful, normal lives in their own neighbor-

hoods, schools and homes; to choose a suitable occupation; and to develop into good, self-sufficient citizens in their communities." The organization was unique because it combined the efforts of government and private agencies, including Denver Public Schools, Denver Rotary Club, and the Colorado Division of Employment, becoming an early example of a highly successful public/private partnership.

The original concept has been credited to Charles E. Greene, chair of the Boys Work Committee and superintendent of Denver Public Schools. Donald Keim was Denver Rotary president at the time, and Frank P. Spratlen served as DBI's first president. Other founding members included T. Chester Hitchings, Denver Boys vice chairman; Harry L. Nicholson, principal of Mitchell school; Harry W. Bundy; Harry H. Cox; Philip X. Daniels; Andrew Dyatt; C. L. Harrington; William R. Humphrey; Robert H. Reeves; and J. Bernard Teetes.

A directorate appointed by Denver Rotary managed the operation. Beginning with voluntary contributions totaling $7,500, and twenty boys, DBI opened its first offices in Maria Mitchell Elementary School, whose principal Harry L. Nicholson also served as the first director. The organization moved to Cole Junior High School in March 1947; both schools were located in a district where juvenile delinquency was a major problem.

"The better part of one's life consists of his friendships."

—Abraham Lincoln

FRANK P. SPRATLEN, is chairman of the board of directors of the active, new organization, Denver Boys, Inc., which Thursday night sponsored a career night for boys in the area served by Annunciation, Cole and Manual schools. The purpose of the program "was not to provide jobs," Spratlen explained, "but to get these boys work-minded." Average age of the boys was fifteen.

CHARLES E. GREENE.   DONALD KEIM.

Denver Boys Inc. (DBI) was founded in the aftermath of World War II to provide a vital kind of friendship: a helping hand for fatherless boys. Denver Boys' first home in 1946 was Maria Mitchell Elementary School. Its principal, Harry L. Nicholson, served as the first director of DBI. The staff also included Robert Colwell, boys' advisor at Cole Junior High School, assistant director; Tom W. Ewing, Baker Jr. High School; Carl M. Dunsworth, Colorado State Employment Service; and Robert S. Herrmann, Denver recreational department. Frank P. Spratlen was the first president of the directorate of the new organization; Charles E. Greene, superintendent of Denver Public Schools, was chairman of the work committee; and Donald Keim was president of the Rotary Club of Denver.

The twelve founders: Harry W. Bundy, Harry H. Cox, Phillip X. Daniels, Andrew Dyatt, Charles E. Greene, C. L. Harrington, T. Chester Hitchings, William R. Humphrey, Harry L. Nicholson, Robert H. Reeves, Frank P. Spratlen, Jr., Bernard Teets, Wesley J. Towne.

ROTARY CLUB LAUNCHES PROGRAM TO AID BOYS

An open house at Cole Junior High School officially launched a program to bring new opportunity to Denver boys under sponsorship of the Denver Rotary Club.

The project is called Denver Boys, Inc., and a full-time staff analyzes problems of boys. The group seeks to solve the boys' troubles by remedying handicaps, finding jobs and providing recreational opportunities.

Rotary members will serve as guides to the boy they are sponsoring.

Harry L. Nicholson, principal of Mitchell School, is director of the project. Various agencies have volunteered the services of three men for full-time work.

Motivating forces behind the new communitywide project, Denver Boys, Inc., to bring new opportunity to Denver boys. A full-time staff, with headquarters at Cole school, analyzes problems of boys. Donald Keim is president of the Rotary club, which is enlisted in the project. Charles E. Greene, superintendent of schools, is chairman of the boys' work committee of the club. They are assisted by Frank T. Spratlen Jr., chairman of the board of directors of Denver Boys, Inc., and T. C. Hitchings, vice chairman of the board.

They are Carl M. Dunsworth, Colorado State Employment Service; Tom W. Ewing, Baker Junior High School teacher, and Robert S. Herrmann, city recreation department specialist.

Spark plugs of the project are Donald Keim, president of Rotary; Charles E. Greene, superintendent of schools and chairman of the boys' work committee of the club; Frank T. Spratlen Jr., chairman of the board of directors of Denver Boys, and T. C. Hitchings, vice chairman of the board.

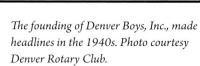

The founding of Denver Boys, Inc., made headlines in the 1940s. Photo courtesy Denver Rotary Club.

In May 1948, after two years of demonstrated success, Denver Boys would be incorporated and take its permanent name. In 1950, the organization relocated again to offices in the Gilpin School Building at 720 Thirtieth Street, expanding to include a staff of six men, three from the Colorado State Employment Office and three from Denver Public Schools, plus one full-time and one part-time secretary paid by Rotary. By this time, DBI had become Denver Rotary's most important community service, providing boys with scholarships to private schools and summer camps, fishing trips, skiing and mountaineering scholarships, and full- and part-time job opportunities. Other services included medical, dental, legal, and psychological assistance, along with contributions for families at Christmas.

Originally, DBI primarily served fatherless boys in elementary school, predelinquent youngsters whose main problem might be poverty, neighborhood environment, truancy, or difficulty getting along with others. Sponsors from Denver Rotary provided support, friendship, and a role model for children sorely in need of help. The sponsor worked with the boy on an individual basis, visiting regularly, and encouraging him to take part in group activities developed by DBI, attending ball games, the Stock Show, and luncheon meetings of the Rotary Club. Sponsors often attended father-son events. The system provided every Rotarian with the opportunity to be part of the organization, which grew steadily, gradually extending its services to boys throughout the city.

CLUB 31 AND POSTWAR DENVER

On August 16, 1945—just two days after the unconditional surrender of Japan marked the end of World War II—Dr. Joyce Stearns of the University of Chicago spoke at a Rotary luncheon. Stearns pointed out the disastrous consequences that would have occurred had the Germans won the race to develop the atomic bomb, and predicted peacetime uses "when the material in a grain of sand would produce enough energy to light an entire city."

Many men stationed in Denver during the war fell in love with the city and returned with their families to make a home. Coupled with returning natives, they

Air travel took off as a means of passenger transportation after World War II. United Airlines jet "Mainliner 300 NC37508" is shown here at Stapleton Airport. Photo courtesy Denver Public Library Western History Department.

created a housing shortage that led to a major building boom and the growth of the suburbs. Once-stagnant Denver politics experienced an unaccustomed jolt as the old guard gave way to a new generation. When young Yale graduate Quigg Newton was elected mayor in 1947, he dragged the reluctant city into the twentieth century. Although Newton had been a Denver Rotarian for years, the relationship between the mayor's office and the organization was never quite as close after his election.

The new mayor made landmark changes, totally reorganizing the municipal government, redrawing City Council boundaries, creating the modern Denver Planning Office and reforming the Department of Health and Hospitals. He also recruited the legendary physician/scientist Florence Sabin in 1948 to revamp the city's health-care plan.

As suburbia blossomed with growing families, Denver gradually morphed into a metropolis, losing some of its charm and much of its provincialism along the way. Denver Rotary would expand along with it, moving into fields of endeavor its founders could never have imagined.

Actress Mae West receives a bouquet of roses from Club President John Sullivan while Frank Ricketson, Jr., looks on (August 21, 1949). "This is my kind of meeting," she quipped. "All men and all hungry." Photo courtesy Denver Rotary Club.

The last Denver streetcar, Trolley No. 65, rode into history in June 1950, marking the end of an era. Photo courtesy Denver Public Library Western History Department.

Rotary is a Lodge without a Ritual, a Religion without a Creed, a Fraternity without a Password and a School without a curriculum.

—*Mile High Keyway*, May 1, 1947

This aerial view of downtown Denver's skyline in 1958 shows the First National Bank Building, Continental Oil Company, Brown Palace Hotel, Mile High Center, Denver Club, Rocky Mountain Telephone Building, Denver Gas and Electric, Republic Building, and Scottish Rite Masonic Temple. Photo courtesy Denver Public Library Western History Department.

CHAPTER IV

Denver Rotary
Grows with the City
1952–1965

THE EMERGING METROPOLIS

On June 10, 1954, Gerald T. Hart, representative of the Murchison Brothers of Dallas, served as Denver Rotary's guest luncheon speaker. During his talk, Hart reported a critical office space shortage and zero-vacancy rate downtown. His company was in the process of constructing one of Denver's first skyscrapers, the twenty-three-story Denver Club Building at 518 Seventeenth Street, which he promised would add more than four hundred thousand square feet to downtown's office space. With a price tag of approximately $8 million, the structure would replace the old brownstone at Seventeenth Street and Glenarm Place, which had been a hub of the Denver social scene since 1881.

The old Denver Club Building at Seventeenth Street and Glenarm Place had been abandoned by May 15, 1953, when this photo was taken. Photo courtesy Denver Public Library Western History Department.

The Petroleum Club Building opened in 1957 at Sixteenth Street and Broadway, accommodating the eleven hundred members of the country's premiere oilman's organization. Other enhancements to the skyline during the period included the twenty-five-story Mile High Center, the Farmer's Union, the Brown Palace Hotel addition (the tallest lightweight concrete building between Chicago and San Francisco), and the Security Life Building.

As a first step toward modernizing the downtown area, Mayor Quigg Newton's administration repealed the twelve-story building height restriction, a 1908 Speer measure intended to preserve an unobstructed view of the Rockies and placate opponents to his ambitious plans for the city. Newton subsequently brought in New York realtor William Zekendorf, who hired Chinese architect I. M. Pei to design the Hilton Hotel and the May D&F Department Store, the result of a merger between the city's two department store giants, the May Company and Daniels and Fisher. A guest speaker at the Denver Rotary luncheon on April 4, 1957, Zekendorf outlined the problems involved with planning a new, revitalized Denver, mainly zoning, rehabilitation, annexation, and coordination between the core city and the suburbs.

The May Company/Daniels and Fisher Department Store merger led to the demolition of the once-sacrosanct five-story Daniels and Fisher Building, although

As mayor, Rotarian Quigg Newton put a new face on Denver and changed the city forever. Photo courtesy Denver Public Library Western History Department.

preservationists managed to save the D&F Tower, which had provided the city's first airplane beacon. The Windsor Hotel would be demolished in 1959 and the Tabor Opera House in 1965, the first rumblings of an urban renewal blitz that would rock the inner city to its core and destroy several downtown landmarks in the process.

The May D&F Entrance Canopy, built in 1959, was the world's longest span hyperbolic paraboloid thin-shell. The building would be demolished in the 1990s. Photo courtesy Denver Public Library Western History Department.

Several Rotary luncheon guest speakers during the 1950s and 1960s, including Bruce Rockwell, chair of the Denver Urban Renewal Authority, addressed the growth issues Denver faced. The most important factor, however, would be water.

Along with a building boom, postwar Denver experienced substantial suburban growth, with housing springing up in former rural areas and farming communities. A drought during the mid-1950s, led to the city's drawing a "blue-pencil" line around Denver that cut off water supply to the suburbs. An article in the April 1965 *Rotarian* described how Denver solved its water problem, at least temporarily, with construction of the Dillon Dam on Blue River and the Roberts Tunnel in 1964.

The Windsor Hotel on Larimer Street, pictured here sometime between 1880 and 1890, would be an early casualty of urban renewal attempts. Once the elegant love nest of silver king Horace Tabor and his mistress, the beautiful Baby Doe, by 1959 it had become a flophouse for transients. Photo courtesy Denver Public Library Western History Department.

The effort would be strongly supported by President Dwight D. Eisenhower (1952–1960), whose wife, Mamie, was a Denver native. "Ike" became quite the local celebrity during the 1950s, visiting Denver often to see his in-laws at 750 Lafayette Street. When Eisenhower had a heart attack in Denver in 1955, he was treated at Fitzsimons Army Hospital. National operations moved out West to a suite at the Brown Palace that became known as "the Denver White House."

The president's support, along with the efforts of Honorary Rotarian Governor Dan Thornton, also helped to bring both the Interstate Highway (I-70) and the Air Force Academy to Colorado. An old-fashioned city booster in the tradition of Robert Speer, Thornton was a walking "Marlboro man" in the days when smoking was still considered sophisticated, sporting a pipe, ten-gallon hat, boots, and an enviable air of confidence. Accused of being an absentee governor and playboy who spent

more time in Hollywood and Washington, D.C., than in Denver, Thornton nevertheless had the charisma and political skills to attract industry to the Rockies.

Denver boomed in the 1950s, adding approximately eighteen hundred residents per month. In less than a decade, the sleepy little city on the plains became a manufacturing and supply depot, production center for Titan missiles and headquarters for scores of businesses in the Rocky Mountain region. And more often than not, Denver Rotarians were the people making it all happen.

A rooftop view of the partially constructed Mile High Center at 1700 Broadway shows nearby buildings, including the Cosmopolitan Hotel, Daniels and Fisher Tower, and the Cooper Building. Photo courtesy Denver Public Library Western History Department.

President Dwight D. Eisenhower made Denver a vacation retreat during his term as president, 1952–1960. His involvement with the state helped pave the way for the I-25 and I-70 super highways. Photo courtesy Denver Public Library Western History Department.

DENVER ROTARY AT MID-CENTURY

Despite the changes in the city skyline, Denver Rotary operations proceeded much as they had for decades. The club still hosted an annual Ladies Night, a picnic at Elitch's, an Orphan's Christmas Party, and a Fun Night for Denver Boys, Inc., at the Twentieth Street Recreation Center. The weekly luncheon meeting began promptly at 12:10, usually in the Silver Glade Room of the Cosmopolitan Hotel, with the

members enthusiastically warbling the *Star Spangled Banner, America the Beautiful,* or *God Bless America.* At each meeting, "Birthatarians" would be recognized and a silver "Denver" dollar awarded to the Rotarian who had traveled the farthest to join the meeting. Installation of officers and directors for the upcoming year took place at the last meeting in June, at which point the identity of the Observer would be revealed to the assembly. (The Observer column in the newsletter, an anonymous and often light-hearted recap of the previous week's gathering, originated in 1933–34, thanks to the creativity of Rotarian Paul B. Lineus.)

In 1961, Rotarian Mark U. Watrous, Colorado's chief highway engineer, stated that the Federal Highway Administration's extension of I-70 across Colorado was "as important to Colorado as the discovery of Gold." This is Colorado's first completed interstate project, which shows sculptured rock slopes and Clear Creek and flyover bridges in the Floyd Hill–Idaho Springs I-70 complex. Photo courtesy Bob Lowdermilk.

Accused of being an absentee governor and playboy who spent more time in Hollywood and Washington, D.C., than in Denver, Governor Dan Thornton (1951–55) nevertheless had the charisma and political skills to attract industry to the Rockies. Photo courtesy Denver Public Library Western History Department.

Christmas for Orphans

THE DENVER POST
PICTURE PAGE

By GENE LINDBERG
Denver Post Staff Writer

SANTA may not get around to the rest of the world till Christmas Eve, but he came early Saturday for the 800 youngsters who attended the Denver Rotary Club's annual Christmas party for orphans at the Centra Theater.

Ten orphanages of the greater Denver area—Catholic, Jewish and Protestant—were represented by boys and girls 3 to 16 years old, with 75 supervisors in charge. More than 60 members of the Rotary Club participated. The youngsters were called for at the orphanages by 12 chartered Denver Tramway Company buses and several private cars.

Arriving at the theater at 9 a.m., they saw a first-run showing of Walt Disney's latest moving picture, "The Castaways," from the Jules Verne story. The picture is booked for a Christmas program at the Denver Theater, but through the courtesy of Fox Theaters and the Disney Distributing Organization the special showing was arranged Saturday.

Police Chief James Slavin provided police supervision. Four clowns from the El Jebel Shrine organization were on hand in full clown uniform—Odie Dunlap, Frank Soper, Francis (Tiny) Eatwell and Frank Van Liew.

More than 1,000 gifts were given, with special presents for the supervisors. There was musical entertainment including Marylin Nelson and her accordion. Dr. Bradford Murphey is president of the Denver Rotary Club. Harry Rosenbaum and Edward W. Thorson were co-chairmen.

Orphanages and homes represented were Colorado State Children's Home, 2305 S. Washington St.; St. Clara's Orphanage, 3800 W. 29th Ave.; St. Vincent's Home for Boys, 4159 Lowell Blvd.; Queen of Heaven Orphanage, 4825 Federal Blvd.; Colorado Christian Home, 4325 W. 29th Ave.; Margery Reed Mayo Day Nursery, 1128 28th St.; Neighborhood House Assn., 1265 Mariposa St.; Clayton College for Boys, 3801 E. 32nd Ave.; Holland Hall for Girls, 1260 Franklin St., and Jewish National Home for Asthmatic Children, 3401 W. 19th Ave.

DENVER POST PHOTOS BY LOWELL GEORGIA

Two open-mouthed youngsters open a present and take a look. Inside the box they found a racing car kit—just one of the some 1,000 gifts given through the efforts of the Rotary.

The Orphans Christmas Party, a Denver Rotary tradition for generations, was held at the Denver Theater in 1962. Photo courtesy The Denver Post.

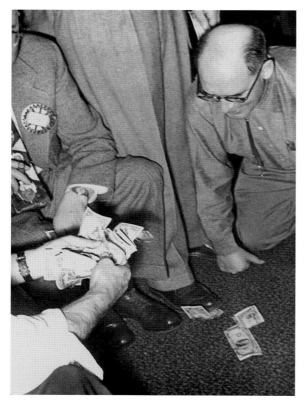

Denver Rotarians are seen here participating in a "fundraiser." Photo courtesy Denver Rotary Club.

The International Services Committee kept the club informed about foreign affairs, particularly the threat of Communism, which seemed to loom over everything during the 1950s and early 1960s. Denver Rotarians were frequently hosts to foreign students and often sent their own children to visit with families overseas.

"I think the best part of Rotary during those years—and today—is the people we meet," said Jim White, discussing a family in France that he and his wife befriended through Rotary in the 1960s. "Alexandre Renaud, who was wartime mayor of Sainte-Mere-Eglise in France, attended our wedding in August 1963. His book, *Sainte Mere Eglis, D-Day 6 June 1944*, a personal account of his experiences, came out in 1984 on the anniversary of the Normandy Invasion. His son, Paul, later had the book translated into English for me and made it available for those Americans attending the 50th Anniversary Celebration in Normandy. The Renaud family and the White family have now had a friendship going since 1955, spanning three generations. My family and I have made many long-lasting international friendships, people I still correspond with today. That's what happens as a result of being a Rotarian—we have connections all over the world."

The meetings recorded in *Mile High Keyway* always had a friendly, folksy tone, reflecting camaraderie among members who called one another by nicknames, often abbreviations of their last names, a.k.a. Saco DeBoer, who fellow Rotarians called "Dee." Businessmen who slunk out of meetings early, or "early risers," would occasionally be chastised, but the Denver club managed to keep its attendance standing in the Top 10 for the Division.

Rotary International celebrated its Golden Anniversary in 1955. This event may have taken place at the Brown Palace. Photo courtesy Denver Rotary.

In 1955, under the administration of President Milton Burnet, Denver Rotary organized the Totem Pole Club for Rotarians who had been members less than six months. The group met once a month at 11:15 a.m., before the regular meeting. Programs usually included a speaker or a film designed to inform new members about the work of Rotary International and the activities of the local club.

THE GOLDEN JUBILEE

Denver Rotary celebrated its Golden Jubilee in 1961, the year that Rotary International accepted Denver's invitation to host the RI convention for the third time in 1966. On June 29, 1961, the membership paid tribute to Wesley J. Towne, Denver Rotary's retiring executive secretary. The oldest living president at the time, Ralph Mayo, Sr., explained tongue in cheek how Towne was hired in January 1934 on a temporary basis "for the princely sum of $175/month" because "the Denver Real Estate Exchange could not afford to keep him." Towne was presented with a diamond pin Rotary lapel button, a watch with the inscription, "For Distinguished Service—The Rotary Club of Denver, 1934–1961," along with a check for $5,000, raised by voluntary contributions from the membership as a retirement gift. Towne remarked that he had worked for twenty-eight presidents, all of whom were "great guys." For many members it signified the end of an era, although the new executive secretary, Dan Paxton, also would serve for many years.

Wesley J. Towne served as the club's executive secretary from 1934 to 1961, under twenty-eight presidents. At his retirement party, he told the group that they all were "great guys." Photo courtesy Denver Rotary Club.

"THE CHIEF COULDN'T COME"

"'JFK and Jackie can't attend the Rotary Party' trumpeted a three-deck headline in *The Denver Post*, 'Voice of the Rocky Mountain Empire.' 'She hasn't a Thing to wear' read a subhead. Rotarians and guests, all 622 of them, found the edition tucked in their places when they filed into the club's recent Golden Anniversary Luncheon. The story, written in a straight-faced manner by *The Denver Post* "Washington Bureau correspondent" caused a sensation. It soon came out, however, that the edition was a stunt by Palmer Hoyt, editor, and the joint committee of the Golden Anniversary Ladies Night program. Rotarian Hoyt replated page 1 and slipped the story into 500 copies of the evening edition."

—*The Rotarian*, May 1962

At the Golden Jubilee meeting at the Hilton Hotel, December 7, 1961, charter member Frank McLister shared his memories of Rotary days past, while Wes Towne provided a history of the Denver Club. Towne reported that during its fifty-year history, Denver Rotary had spent a total of $239,651 on Denver Boys, Inc., and the scholarship program and contributed $6,381 to RI's Foundation Fellowship for International Understanding.

Of the fifty-two presidents to date, eight had served as district governors from the Denver Club and two from other clubs before they moved to Denver. They included: District 14: John E. Zahn, 1915–16; District 21: William R. McFarland, 1918–19; District 7: Harry C. Brown, M.D., 1925–26; Findlay L. McFarland, 1931–32; George W. Olinger, 1934–35; Roy J. Weaver (Pueblo), 1936–37; Mortimer Stone (Fort Collins), 1938–39; District 113: P. Hicks Cadle, 1944–45; District 168: John McMurtrey, 1954–55; and Ray Jenkins, 1959–60. Brown, Olinger, Weaver, Cadle, Gratton E. Hancock, and D. D. Monroe had served as directors of RI.

ROTARY EXTENDS YOUTH PROGRAMS

In conjunction with Denver Rotary's Golden Anniversary, on September 28, 1961, *Mile High Keyway* announced the reorganization of the Boys Work Committee, which had been renamed the Scholarship and Achievement Committee. Denver Rotary extended its support to both boys and girls that year. In 1966, the Junior League of Denver and Zonta Women's Club of Denver founded Denver Girls, to which Denver Rotary later added its support. Denver Boys and Denver Girls merged in 1993 to become Denver Kids, Inc.

The new group overseeing all youth work included a College Scholarship Coordinating Committee, a Scholarship and Achievement Award Committee, a Rotary Loan Fund Committee, a Nurses Assistance Committee, the Denver Boys, Inc. Board, Sponsor for Girls Committee, and the Orphans Theater Party Committee. The Scholarship and Achievement Award would be available for both boys and girls, with the $25 scholarship and $20 achievement award granted to students in need in tenth through twelfth grades. Denver Boys, Inc., received $11,097, the larger share of the budget, while $5,000 was allocated to the Scholarship and Award Committee.

Children pose with Denver Mayor Thomas G. Currigan (1963–1968), in his office at the City and County Building. They stand in front of a table covered with political posters featuring Richard Nixon, Spiro Agnew, and even Hubert Humphry. Photo courtesy Denver Public Library Western History Department.

MOVERS AND SHAKERS

Over the preceding decades, Denver Rotary became one of the largest clubs in the world, boasting 478 members by 1960. The club attracted super achievers in multiple realms including business, law, journalism, and finance. Even future Supreme Court Judge Byron "Whizzer" White joined in 1959 while practicing law in Denver. Other high-powered Rotarians included *Denver Post* editor and publisher Palmer Hoyt (joined in Oregon, 1932), who kept Denver Rotary activities in the public eye. Hired by owner Helen Bonfils in 1946 to infuse new life into the stodgy, conservative newspaper, Hoyt was one of the most influential journalists Denver has ever produced, turning the *Post* into a Pulitzer Prize-winner. Under Hoyt's management, *The Denver Post* became one of the first newspapers in the country to actively oppose the communist witch-hunts of Sen. Joe McCarthy and one of the first to support the Civil Rights movement. By establishing a connection with the community and an international perspective, Hoyt turned the *Post* into the voice of the Rocky Mountain West.

On April 29, 1958, the club paid homage to the recently deceased Rotarian Louis F. Eppich, a prominent realtor, former club president (1933–34), and a Rotarian since July 1922. Among his many achievements, Eppich had been instrumental in securing $50,000 in Federal Aid funding for the survey that resulted in Denver's first interstate highway, I-25, originally dubbed the Valley Highway because it ran along the South Platte Valley. Called "the father of zoning," Eppich had been instrumental in creation of the Denver Planning Department and development of the Mountain Parks System and Red Rocks.

Louis F. Eppich, former club president (1933–34), was instrumental in securing $50,000 in Federal-Aid funding for the survey that resulted in Denver's first Interstate Highway, I-25. Originally dubbed the Valley Highway because it ran along the South Platte Valley, the thoroughfare opened on November 23, 1958. Photo courtesy Bob Lowdermilk.

Third-generation Rotarian Armin P. (Pete) Thebus, who joined Denver Rotary Club April 11, 1957, recalled: "In those days, we had quite a few accountants, lawyers and many more entrepreneurs than today. We had the company heads as members— 'Ma' Bell, Public Service Company, eight car dealerships, eight airlines, all the bank presidents, all leaders of community. There was a camaraderie here that made things

By the early 1960s, Fourteenth and Larimer Streets had become Denver's skid row. Photo courtesy Denver Public Library Western History Department.

Will F. Nicholson, seen here with his wife, Gladys, served a term as Denver mayor during the Valley Highway construction, 1955–59. Photo courtesy Denver Public Library Western History Department.

On June 10, 1965, a young developer named Dana Crawford enthusiastically pitched "the exciting new Larimer Square project" to Denver Rotary. Crawford made the first move in the attempt to save historic downtown buildings from demolition. Photo courtesy Denver Public Library Western History Department.

happen. Denver Rotarians lived in the city and ran the city. If you needed something, you knew who to call, but the club itself didn't get too much involved in politics."

At that time, according to Rotarian Jim McFall (1967), only the top executives of corporations were solicited for membership in Rotary, which still recruits members by invitation only. "You had to be 'tapped,'" he said. "After your name had been submitted, two or three others would have to support you before you could be considered for membership."

"We were somewhat elitist in those days and we had a crazy classification system," said Jim Wilkins, who prides himself on being the only member who was ever asked to resign and later became president (1994–95). "I originally joined in 1978 under the classification 'Sales Management,'" he explained. "When I switched careers and became a lowly real estate agent, Dan Paxton told me that the classification was full and I had to leave. Fortunately they changed the rules not too long after that."

"Visitors to Denver stood in line to speak at the club, and we've never had to pay anyone," said Thebus. Prominent guests included Secretary of State Henry Cabot Lodge, Hollywood fashion expert Edith Head (who caught the Asian flu and had to send her top designer), historian Arnold J. Toynbee, actor Henry Fonda, and local politicians and celebrities including CU football coach Everett John "Sonny" Grendelius, Colorado Governor John A. Love, and preservationist/developer Dana Crawford, who advised the group on June 10, 1965, about "The Exciting Larimer Square Project."

Thebus, who served as sergeant-at-arms since his earliest Rotary days, admits to being somewhat intimidated by the prestigious crowd at first. "I was very young when I joined, and here were all these civic leaders and heads of businesses. I thought they would be stuffy, but when I got to know them better, they turned out to be pretty nice guys. We even had a bowling league." The Denver Businessman's Bowling League, which celebrated its fortieth anniversary in 1961, included the Lions, Lions Cubs, Kiwanis, Civitan, Sertoma, Optimist, and Exchange. The group met Monday evenings at the 20th Century Lanes at 1241 Broadway.

GROWTH OF DENVER ROTARY, 1911–1960

ABBREVIATION OF A CHART PUBLISHED IN MILE HIGH KEYWAY, SEPTEMBER 8, 1960

YEAR	DENVER	RI CLUBS	ROTARIANS WORLDWIDE
1911–12	60	49	5,008
1915	146	167	20,700
1920	194	758	55,150
1925	217	2,096	108,000
1930	234	3,349	153,000
1935	277	3,842	161,000
1940	322	5,066	214,000
1945	348	5,441	247,200
1950	418	7,113	342,000
1955	435	8,780	419,000
1960	478	10,701	495,500

A NEW CLUB IN DENVER?

The first indication that a new club might be chartered within the Denver city limits came in summer 1964, when *Keyway* announced a debate on the topic scheduled for July 30, followed by a vote on August 6. Rotary International encouraged the formation of new clubs in large cities that contained "one or more well-defined commercial trade centers," and the new Cherry Creek Shopping Center (1953) created by Rotarian Temple Buell and University Hills Shopping Center (1955) certainly qualified. The Board appointed a committee consisting of Directors Hatfield Chilson and Gene Frink to advocate the affirmative side of the issue and Van Holt Garrett, Jr., and Tom Tierney to present the negative.

The proposed boundaries for the new club, east of University Boulevard and south of Sixth Avenue, included the town of Glendale and the adjoining unincorporated Arapahoe County. District Governor Erniel Altick had indicated that he would favor the move, and the Rotary Club of Englewood agreed to serve as sponsor. Even so, Denver Rotary had to approve the measure. Apparently the new club would have only 15 members, who could also retain membership in the parent club.

When the 359 ballots were counted on August 6, 121 members had voted for the resolution and 238 against. The Rotary Club of University Hills would not be charted until October 6, 1971, under the leadership of President Peter Bowes, who at thirty-three became the youngest Denver Rotary president in the club's history.

We make a living by what we get, we make a life by what we give.

—Denver Rotarian Will Schweigert, May 3, 1966

In keeping with the 1966 RI Convention theme "Build for the Future," guest speakers included Secretary
of State Dean Rusk; Lord Caradon (Hugh Mackintosh Foot), Great Britain's representative to the
United Nations; and U.S. astronaut L. Gordon Cooper. Photo courtesy Denver Rotary Club.

CHAPTER V

Building for the Future
1966–1979

DENVER WELCOMES THE 1966 CONVENTION

As Denver Rotary prepared for the third Rotary International Convention in forty years, local newspapers noted that the city had nearly doubled in size since the first gathering in 1926. By 1966, traffic buzzed through Denver on Interstate Highways 25 and 70 (still under construction) and the city could boast a handful of skyscrapers, a blossoming Colorado ski industry, a team in the American Football League, and even a tropical conservatory at Denver Botanic Gardens. After the disastrous South Platte River flood the previous summer, Denverites approved construction of the Chatfield Dam and Reservoir to protect the city from subsequent multimillion-dollar water disasters.

This view of the central business district between 1960 and 1970 shows the Mile High Center, Cosmopolitan Hotel, Brown Palace Hotel, Continental Oil Building, Trinity Methodist Church, the Scottish Rite Masonic Temple, Security Life Building, and a parking garage ramp. Sign on Petroleum Club building reads "Conoco." Other signs read "Denver United States National Bank," and "Brown Palace Hotel." Photo courtesy Denver Public Library Western History Department.

The South Platte Flood of 1965 did millions of dollars worth of damage and motivated the construction of Chatfield Dam. Photo courtesy Denver Public Library Western History Department.

In some ways, the late 1950s and early 1960s marked the last hurrah for the old Denver power elite. Although their descendants intermarried enthusiastically to keep the wealth in the family (notably the Cheesman, Evans, and Boettcher crowd), the giants were fading fast: Ben Stapleton died in 1950, Gerald Hughes and Claude Boettcher in 1957, and Lawrence Phipps in 1958. Echoing their demise, landmarks of yesteryear crashed in clouds of dust that blanketed the city for years. As a result, by the mid-1970s, the city had lost much of its small town flavor.

The tumultuous era that began with the 1963 assassination of President John F. Kennedy continued well beyond President Richard Nixon's resignation in 1974. Among the positives, the Civil Rights movement, which had stagnated since World War II, accelerated at an incredible pace, leading to sweeping reform legislation that changed the face of American society. When the *Swann v. Charlotte-Mecklenburg Board of Education* Supreme Court decision made busing of students mandatory in 1971, however, many disgruntled Denverites fled to the suburbs.

By 1966, Vietnam had already escalated into a full-scale war and "flower power" was budding in San Francisco. *The Rotarian* mentioned that the 1966 Convention wore the face of youth, with an unprecedented number of younger people attending; 1,845 unpaid registrants signified a healthy representation by family members under sixteen. These future Rotarians congregated in the area they called the "Kiva," below the three-thousand-seat theater next door to the auditorium, and held their own mini-convention.

THE PARTY COMES TO TOWN

Beginning in early June 1966, billboards, bunting and balloons (150,000 courtesy of the May D&F Department Store) announced the imminent deluge of approximately fifteen thousand Rotarians into the city. Ray Jenkins, chair of the Host Club Housing Committee, booked 150 local hotels and motels for visitors and pleaded with members to open their homes for informal gatherings. "It isn't necessary to make a steak dinner out of the thing," he added. "If you wanted to broil hamburgers in the backyard, this would be highly acceptable. This is America!"

Rotarian Peter Bowes recalled that he got involved with the convention because one of the co-chairs happened to be his father's fraternity brother, Richard Wright.

Until 1982, Sixteenth Street was still open to traffic, and those who grew up in Denver may recall "cruising Sixteenth Street" as teenagers on a Saturday night. In this photo, taken during the late 1960s, the pre-mall thoroughfare is decked out for the holidays. Photo courtesy Denver Public Library Western History Department.

Many antiwar protests took place in Denver during the Vietnam War, including this one on East Colfax Avenue in 1971. Photo courtesy Tom Noel.

"It was a lot of fun and quite an undertaking," Bowes said. "I had only been in Rotary for three years, so I was just an assistant. I did various small jobs, sometimes acting as a courier. My wife and I went to the convention the year before in Atlantic City, where we ran a booth and handed out flyers and carnations."

On June 11, the conventioneers and their families congregated at Red Rocks to celebrate the park's Twenty-fifth Anniversary. Interestingly, the program echoed the 1941 gala, featuring opera stars from the Met, the Dallas Rotary Chorus, and the Koshare Indian Dancers, the Boy Scouts of La Junta, who performed an Eagle Ceremonial Dance. (*Rotarian* reporter Ivan Doig dutifully reported that, "at least one in ten *were* actually Indians.") The following evening, 375 members of the Mormon Tabernacle Choir wowed conventioneers at the Denver Auditorium, which was decked out with flags from 133 countries.

Dr. Robert Stearns, head of the Welcoming Committee made sure that waitresses, store clerks, and even policemen wore their "Welcome Rotarians" buttons. Stearns cut quite a figure in certain circles, serving at various times as president of Denver Rotary in 1956–57, both the Denver and the Colorado Bar Associations, the University of Colorado, the Boettcher Foundation, and director of the Webb-Waring Institute for Medical Research.

With Stearns at the helm, the city pulled out all the stops to entertain visitors that week. A rodeo at the Coliseum opened with the young Westernaires of Jefferson County, who rode out the flags from Rotary nations. Bandleader Wayne King entertained at the President's Ball, while prominent guest speakers at the convention included Secretary of State Dean Rusk; Lord Caradon (Hugh Mackintosh Foot), Great Britain's representative to the United Nations; and U.S. astronaut L. Gordon Cooper. In keeping with the convention theme, "Build for the Future," Rusk took the opportunity to promote the North Atlantic Treaty Organization (N.A.T.O.), while Cooper showed a film on the space program. The United States would win the "space race" three years later by being first to put a man on the moon.

Rotary wives and daughters enjoyed tea with Ann Love, the governor's wife, and the proverbial fashion show. Ray Jenkins, later elected district governor, and Denver Rotary President Tom Tierney were asked to wear porters' outfits and carry luggage for the ladies for the event. Tierney was heard to remark, "I wish I was dead."

Convention ceremonies ended traditionally, with Cooper leading conventioneers in a chorus of *Auld Lang Syne*. For months afterward, Denver Rotarians received letters from around the world thanking their hosts for the hospitality. Interestingly, the situation in Southeast Asia that would make headlines within a few years received minimal attention during the convention.

BIRTH OF THE DENVER ROTARY CLUB FOUNDATION

The Rotary International Foundation had emerged from the June 1917 Rotary International Convention in Atlanta, Georgia. While World War I raged in Europe, President Arch Klumph of Cleveland suggested that the organization form "an endowment for doing good in the world, in charitable, educational, and other avenues."

"I think they had about $26.50 profit left over from the convention," chuckles Grant Wilkins, Denver Rotary president in 1978–79. "Humble beginnings, but money went a lot further in those days. The fund didn't really grow until after Paul Harris died, and people began contributing to the foundation in his memory. That's when it really took off."

In 1969, Dan Paxton, the club's executive director proposed the formation of a Denver Rotary Club Foundation similar to those organized by other larger clubs around the country. "The RI foundation was working on international projects, but we thought there was an equal need in Denver for local projects, for youth, senior citizens, etc.," said Wilkins. The tax-exempt organization would also be helpful in channeling bequests from wills, trusts, insurance policies, and contributions and donations.

With the strong support of President (Dr.) John H. Amisse, 1968–69, Denver Rotary gave the new Foundation a nod of approval on March 6, 1969. Three months later, Ralph Johnson, Dwight Phelps, Ralph Mayo, retired Rear Admiral Charles J. McWhinnie, and Dick Davis, the club's current president, signed incorporation papers. Initially, Denver Rotary provided only a small operating budget of $100/year.

Rotarians attend a meeting with Kiyosi "George" Togasaki, Rotary International president, 1968–69. Seated, left to right, are unidentified Rotarian; Ray Jenkins, Denver Rotary Club president, 1957–58; RI President Togasaki; and George R. Means, general secretary of Rotary International, 1953–1972. Back row, left to right, are unidentified Rotarian; Dick Wright, Denver Rotary Club president, 1959–1960; Shelby Harper, Denver Club president, 1963–64; Bob Stearns, Denver Rotary president, 1956–57; and two unidentified individuals. Wright and Harper would both be instrumental in the formation of the Auraria Higher Education Center. Photo courtesy Denver Rotary Club.

THE FIRST MAJOR DONATION TO THE FOUNDATION

On December 4, 1972, *Mile High Keyway* announced that Ed Kassler, Jr., had provided a jumpstart for the fledgling Denver Rotary Club Foundation. The entrepreneurial creator of the Kassler Mortgage Company in 1924, the realtor made his company a leader in the field before selling the business in 1964. A community near Highlands Ranch still bears his name.

Kassler, a generous supporter of the Boys Work fund and an enthusiastic Rotarian, promised to contribute $12,500 to the Foundation with the stipulation that members would provide a match in gifts or pledges. By January 15, 1973, the newsletter announced that $6,209 had already been received, with an additional $325 in pledges promised. One member donated $400 in stocks, maintaining that "the certificates were just lying around in the bottom of his portfolio, which he wanted to clean out." *Keyway* subsequently announced: "IF YOU HAVE ANY STOCKS MESSING UP YOUR PORTFOLIO, WE'LL SELL THEM FOR YOU, PRONTO!"

Before Kassler died on September 23, 1973, he wrote a check (he had donated $10,000 up front) to fulfill his promise, even though the membership was still short of the match.

THE DAN PAXTON SOCIETY

On April 10, 1977, Denver Rotary suffered the loss of Dan C. Paxton, the club's longtime unofficial leader. A Colorado native from Durango, Paxton had

been executive secretary of the St. Louis Rotary for fifteen years before accepting a position in Denver in 1961. Thanks to his efforts, the *St. Louis Pepper Box* became one of Rotary's best publications, an effort he duplicated with *Mile High Keyway*. Known for his cheerful disposition along with his efficiency, Paxton was popular with most Rotarians. During his tenure, the title of his position changed from executive secretary to executive director as the club grew and his duties expanded.

Rotarians who knew Paxton personally, including Pete Thebus, Bill Diss, and Jim McFall, remember him as "a force of nature." According to Jim White, "Dan

Dan Paxton (left) poses with (right to left) Ralph Johnson and Dr. John Amess, Rotary president, 1968–69. The individual standing on Paxton's immediate left has not been identified. Photo courtesy Denver Rotary Club.

Jim White's family enjoys a Rotary Christmas party in 1978. Left to right: Jim's son Scott (now a Denver Rotarian); his nephew Chad; his brother Joe White (district governor in Pennsylvania); Jim's parents, La Veda and Ed White; Jim's son Eric (also a Denver Rotarian); Jim White and daughter Tanya center front. Jim's wife Lee was in the hospital during this party. "She was always present in spirit," Jim said. Photo courtesy Jim White.

Paxton actually told the presidents what to do. When he wanted them to do something, he would convince them it was their idea!"

On May 20, 1977, the Rotary Board voted to restructure the Denver Rotary Foundation, establishing a nine-member Board of Trustees appointed to two, four, and six-year terms. Bill Hornby would be the first president, with Junius Baxter, Ray Jenkins, Rabbi Earl Stone, Roger L. Kinney, Robert S. McCollum, Dr. Robert B. Sawyer, Kenneth W. Caughey, John R. Dickinson, and John C. Mitchell serving as trustees.

At that meeting, Preston Smith (president 1977–78) suggested the adoption of a Dan Paxton Society in memory of the late executive director. Members could contribute by 1) an outright gift of $1,000; 2) a $5,000 bequest in a will or insurance policy; 3) a sustaining membership of $100/year; or 4) $25 added to monthly dues until the amount reached $1,000.

By March 17, 1978, the Dan Paxton Society claimed eighty-three members and the Foundation set its first goal at $1 million. *Mile High Keyway* subtly reminded readers, "YOU OUGHT TO BE A PART OF THIS!"

Steve Dowson (left) and Jim White tend bar during a regional meeting at the Broadmoor. According to White, Temple Buell preferred beer, so he brought it himself. Photo courtesy Denver Rotary Club.

ROTARACT CLUB FORMS AT THE UNIVERSITY OF DENVER

On February 27, 1969, *Mile High Keyway* proudly announced the birth of the first Rotaract Club at the University of Denver. Partly in response to growing social unrest at universities around the country, RI President Luther Hodges approved the first Rotaract Club for young people in North Charlotte, North Carolina, on March 13, 1968. The name *Rotaract* ("Rotary in Action") signified the affiliation with both Rotary and the Interact Clubs, also formed in the 1960s for mini-Rotarians ages fourteen to eighteen.

According to *Mile High Keyway*, the idea for a Denver club began to take shape in April 1968. Denver Rotarian Dr. Lew Barbato chaired the initial D.U. organizational meeting and quickly turned over the gavel to the club's first president, Harold Smethills, Jr., the offspring of Denver Rotary District Governor Harold R. Smethills, 1958–59. (More than fulfilling his promise as a student, Harold, Jr., later became an executive at United Banks of Colorado and VP/CEO of the Coors Company, leading the spin-off of nonbrewery businesses into a Fortune 500 company.)

Tale of two presidents: Rotary Club President Preston Smith, 1977–78, welcomes former U.S. President Gerald Ford. Photo courtesy Denver Rotary Club.

Rotaract clubs were committed to constructive social change, leadership and high ethical standards. When the D.U. group spoke at a Rotary luncheon, the Observer remarked, "It is a great thing to hear young men talk and act like this in a day when violence seems to be so much in the limelight." The D.U. Rotaract was for men only, although such groups were open to women at the option of the sponsor. Today, both sexes may join. Members are students and young professionals in their early twenties focused on local volunteer service, leadership, professional development, international understanding, and goodwill.

DENVER'S FIRST PAUL HARRIS FELLOWS

On January 21, 1974, *Mile High Keyway* sent an SOS to the membership bemoaning the lack of a Paul Harris Fellow in Denver Rotary. The advantages to a District were numerous, the newsletter maintained. Rotary Districts were allotted awards such as group study exchanges and postgraduate and undergraduate fellowships based on how much money the district contributed to the Rotary International Foundation. Basically, Denver Rotarians were advised to "do the math."

For each $1,000 contributed to the RI Foundation, someone (generally the donor or a family member) would be designated a fellow. At the February 21, 1973 meeting, club secretary Roger Kinney announced that Dr. Everette Peterson (dentist, longtime president of the Denver Executives Club); Chandler Weaver (engineer, oil man) and Ray Jenkins (zone manager of Rocky Mountain J. C. Penney Company) had become Denver's first Paul Harris fellows. They

would soon be joined by architect Temple Buell. *Mile High Keyway* noted that Peterson had been first to contribute toward a match for Kessler's donation to the Denver Rotary Foundation. Jenkins, a former Denver Rotary president in 1957–58, district governor in 1959–60, and RI director in 1963–65, received his fellowship as a birthday gift from his wife, Gayle. The following month, on his wife's birthday, Jenkins returned the favor. Later they purchased fellowships for Gayle's two sons, Rike and John Robert (Bob) Wootten. Rike became president of the Denver Rotary Club Foundation in 2004–05, while Bob joined clubs in Oklahoma City, Dallas, and El Paso, later becoming governor of District 5520, which included New Mexico and West Texas.

In 1977, Denver Rotary established the Ray Jenkins Award, given annually to the club in Rotary District 5450 with the highest per capita contribution to Rotary International Foundation for the year.

WORKING WITH DENVER BOYS

Rotary continued and expanded Denver Boys, Inc., during the late 1960s and 1970s. By 1969, the program required an annual budget of $100,000, $14,000 of which Rotary provided for staff salaries, office management, and a camping fund. Five years later, the organization would serve 254 students in forty-six elementary schools, fifteen junior high schools, and seven high schools. Programs expanded to include both a fall and spring picnic at Sloan Lake, a 10th Mountain Division ski program, a Denver Broncos football clinic, plus the annual Fun Night and camping scholarships.

Rotarian Jim McFall sponsored two Denver Boys from age ten until they were about seventeen, an experience he calls rewarding and sometimes difficult. "Not everybody liked the program, but I thought it was great," he said. "I would pick the boy up once a month on Saturdays and we would do different things. Often I would include him in family activities like sledding trips in the foothills or working in the garden. The goal was to give him a time to talk. Sometimes the mother would be helpful, and sometimes she wasn't. One of my boys was the illegitimate son of a prominent banker, and in those days, that was a stigma. The family always had money, but his father never acknowledged the child or got involved in his life.

"Denver Boys made us realize how fragile all of our lives really are," he continued. "Being raised by single mothers—it could have happened to any one of us."

DENVER GIRLS, INC.

In 1966, a task force from Ladies of Rotary and the Zonta Club, an international organization of businesswomen, approached the Denver Public Schools with the possibility of establishing a program for girls similar to Denver Boys, Inc. As the plan developed, the Junior League of Denver and Zonta International became the sponsoring organizations, eventually joined by Denver Rotary.

Like Denver Boys, Inc., the program would be open to children ages ten to seventeen, recommended by school faculty, teachers, social workers, etc. These girls were at risk of dropping out of school and came from homes where education was not a priority. Denver Public Schools would provide a coordinator who would work closely with school personnel to screen and find individuals most likely to benefit from a one to one relationship outside the home. The sponsoring organizations would hire a secretary to handle the office work and Denver Public Schools would provide the office space.

After a test run, Denver Girls, Inc., formally opened its doors in 1970. Along with flexible counseling services, the organization helped with employment if the girls were old enough to work, medical or dental assistance, opportunities to attend social and cultural events otherwise beyond their means and scholarship assistance. Offices were located at Fairmont Elementary School on West Third Avenue.

ADAPTING TO A NEW ERA

The social changes that were sweeping the nation began to impact Denver Rotary in 1966, when the club quietly welcomed its first African American member, Dr. Sebastian C. Owens, executive director of the Urban League Colorado. Owens became a Denver Rotary Club Board director in 1970–1972, and the club's second vice president in 1971–72. He would be followed by James H. Jenks in 1968, manager of Process Engineering for Samsonite; Reverend Murphy C. Williams in 1969, pastor of New Hope Baptist Church; and Dr. William A. Bowers in 1970, podiatrist.

On January 15, 1973, Club 31 welcomed Floyd Douglas Little, an African American and the first Denver Bronco to join the club. A three-time All-American halfback at Syracuse University, 1964–66, Little became the first No. 1 draft pick to sign with the Broncos. Nicknamed "The Franchise," Floyd Little helped to keep the team in Denver and convince voters to approve funds for Mile High Stadium. (Editorials by Bill Hornby at *The Denver Post* also encouraged Denverites to fund the $20 million stadium, which was replaced by Invesco Field at Mile High in

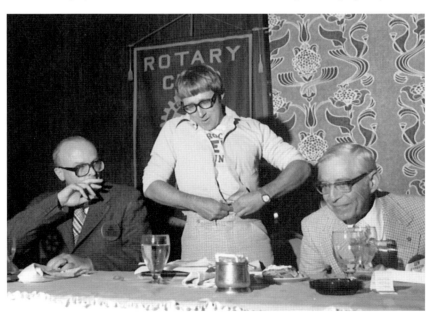

Club President Bill Hornby (1976–77), left, suppresses a grin as secretary and future Denver Rotary president Jim Warner (in female garb) proceeds to disrobe. Lew Barbato is seated right. Photo courtesy the Knight family.

DENVER BOYS AND DENVER GIRLS MADE THE DIFFERENCE

LUIS VILLEREAL,
FOUNDER OF SAVE OUR YOUTH

"I was one of four brothers who were all Denver Boys," said Villereal. "I joined when I was twelve or thirteen, mostly because my older brother Robert belonged. We each had a counselor from the school, but I was closest to my volunteer sponsor, a remarkable person named Max Coats. He was a Rotarian, a chemical engineer, and CEO at ARCO Chemical plant and a very bright man. He basically decided to invest part of his life in me, to give me encouragement and push me to achieve. He began mentoring me when I was in middle school at Skinner Junior High, through my years at North High School, and even while I was in graduate school. In fact, we maintained our friendship up until the time he passed away.

"I lost my father when I was nine, and like all fatherless boys, I was looking for a replacement," he said. "For me, introducing a caring male into my life was the most important benefit of Denver Boys."

In 1993, after obtaining a master's degree in social work, Villereal founded a mentoring program in Denver similar to Denver Boys, Inc., called "Save Our Youth," which works with about 450 boys on a one-to-one basis. Villereal's brothers also benefited from the program. One became a "blue ribbon" school principal with a Ph.D. in education, while another is dean of students at East High School. The fourth brother recently retired from the Denver Water Department.

"I think all young people reflect the people they've been connected to," he added. "Children live up to the expectation of caring adults."

CLARICY WEEAMS,
SIGN LANGUAGE INTERPRETER

"I became involved in Denver Girls when I was in seventh grade at Cole Middle School," Weeams recalled. "At the time, I was having problems with peer pressure. My parents are deaf, so that was another dynamic I had to deal with. Luckily, someone recommended me to Denver Girls Program. A counselor would come to the school to see how I was doing and make sure I got some one-on-one time.

"The volunteer, Kathy Soakes, was a teacher and a homemaker, and she and I became good friends. She took me to luncheons and fashion shows, and I was asked to speak to Denver Rotary about my experiences with the organization.

"I think that being involved with Denver Girls gave me role models, helped me set goals, and showed me how my life could improve. I kept in touch with my counselor in the program over the years.

Weeams worked for the Denver Water Department as a bookkeeper for twenty-one years. Later she returned to finish college and is now a sign language interpreter.

CHARLES EMMONS,
COLLEGE BOOK STORE MANAGER

"My father passed when I was three, and luckily my mom found the program through the school system. At that time I was attending Whittier Elementary School in third grade, and I also had an older brother in Denver Boys.

"A senior counselor would see me during the school year, every two weeks or so, and I had a volunteer sponsor. I really appreciated someone being concerned about my well-being, and the program gave me numerous opportunities. My brother and I would go to sporting events like Denver Broncos football games and Denver Bears baseball games, and I had the chance to go to Wilderness Camp in Vail. I learned to ski through a partnership with Denver Boys and the 10th Mountain Division, and later I went through Outward Bound.

"When I was in junior high, I had problems with peers. School and good grades were important to me, which was something my peers didn't care about. Through Denver Boys, I had the opportunity to attend Denver Country Day School, which gave me a different perspective than public schools."

Emmons finished college out of state and then returned to Denver. He is currently a manager at the Auraria Book Center. Both he and his brother served on the Board of Directors at Denver Boys, and Emmons worked on the public relations committee and edited the organization's newsletter. He has sponsored two boys, who he liked to take skiing to Loveland and Winter Park.

"I think that the program really opens up your world," he said. "You learn that you're not just confined to your neighborhood."

September 2001.) Little played for the Broncos from 1969 to 1975, leading the NFL in rushing in 1971 and touchdowns in 1973. While playing professionally in Denver, he earned a master's degree in judicial administration and became involved with many local charities. A well-known public speaker, he often told his audience: "God gave you two ends, one to sit on, one to think with. Heads you win, tails you lose." Little was inducted into the Pro Football Hall of Fame on August 7, 2010, following in the footsteps of quarterback John Elway and offensive tackle Gary Zimmerman.

The other social revolution of the decade, the Feminist Movement, had little impact on the always-chivalrous Denver Rotarians, whose wives and daughters contributed much to the organization. During the 1960s and 1970s, *Mile High Keyway* would occasionally publish a letter from a grateful young woman who had received a scholarship or a Denver Girl who had benefited from the program. Female guest speakers were nothing new, and occasionally a report or article might be written by a woman. If anyone ever suggested that women join the club, however, no mention was ever made in the newsletter.

Change was in the wind as early as 1976–77, however. The Membership Directory that year began with a listing of all Ladies of the Denver Rotary presidents since 1927–28. Significance might be gleaned from the groundbreaking inclusion of their first names, i.e., Mrs. Elliott Houston (Betty) in 1927–28. Until the 1970s, even newspapers rarely used a woman's first name unless she was a widow.

At least it was a start.

DENVER ROTARY LAUNCHES THE FIRST SATELLITE CLUB

Although a club at University Hills had already been voted down twice, President Peter Bowes, 1970–71, wanted to give it another try. "I was only thirty-three when I became president, and I think I was representative of a younger generation that was more open to new ideas," he said. "Also, Rotary International was always big on promoting extension of clubs, making the experience available to more people," he said "Actually, they hoped to put a club wherever they wanted one, but that never happened. In spring of 1970, a motion went before the membership to give RI that authority, but 60 percent of members voted against it.

"I think early efforts to form another club in Denver failed because the issue would be subject to a major debate each time. People got emotional and proprietary and raised irrelevant and insignificant issues. When I became president, I asked a small group of five or six people to study the facts and make a recommendation. There was no open forum."

On April 15, 1971, the Denver Rotary Board of Directors presented a resolution to amend the Constitution and release the area south of Louisiana Avenue and east of High Street for a new club. Letters of opposition would be published in the April 26 *Mile High Keyway*. Without written objection, a vote on April 29 approved the measure by an overwhelming 307 to 29. The new club held its kickoff meeting in July. Denver Rotary would subsequently cede territory to sponsor other clubs, including Denver Cherry Creek in 1987 and Denver Mile High in 1989.

KEEPING IT LIGHT

Since the first Rotarian cracked the first joke, nearly every program or newsletter contained a touch of humor, no matter how dire the world situation. The offering for March 12, 1973:

"And now, gentlemen," continued the congressman, "I wish to tax your memories."

"Good heavens," muttered a colleague, "Why haven't we thought of this before?"

ROTARIANS TO REMEMBER

Rotarian David French and Wally Hultin, husband of Denver Rotarian Donna Hultin, remodeled the old D&F Tower into condominiums. Photo courtesy Carl Lindsay.

As president of the Colorado Historical Society Board from 1959–69, lawyer Stephen Hart guided the organization through acquisition of regional museums, including the Grant Humphreys mansion and the Byers-Evans house, and development of Georgetown Historic Mining and Railroad District. The History Colorado Center Library is named in his honor. Photo courtesy History Colorado Center.

BYRON R. "WHIZZER" WHITE
(Joined 1959. Classification: Law, Oil and Gas)

On February 12, 1976, the club celebrated the "homecoming" of Supreme Court Chief Justice Byron R. "Whizzer" White, a former Denver Rotarian and Fort Collins native. Always a brilliant student, White won a scholarship to the University of Colorado, where he graduated at the top of his class. During senior year, he was student body president and a football, basketball, and baseball star, dubbed "Whizzer White" by the press, who made him a national hero.

After college, White played professionally for the Pittsburgh Pirates (now the Pittsburgh Steelers) and the Detroit Lions, becoming the highest-paid player in pro football ($15,000/year in 1938 equals $232,500 in 2010 dollars) and winning a spot in the National Pro Football Hall of Fame. The following year he attended Oxford on a Rhodes scholarship when his studies were interrupted by World War II. He subsequently won two Bronze Stars during his stint in the Navy.

From 1947 until 1961, White was a member of the Denver law firm Davis, Graham, and Stubbs. After racking up "a brilliant attendance record," at Rotary, according to *Mile High Keyway*, he helped with John F. Kennedy's presidential campaign in the West. Kennedy subsequently appointed him U.S. deputy attorney general, second in command to Robert Kennedy. White took the field as a leading player in desegregation efforts, personally facing down Alabama Governor John Patterson, who was in league with the Ku Klux Klan. A grateful president who knew talent when he saw it, Kennedy named White to the Supreme Court in 1962, where he served for the next thirty-one years.

STEPHEN HARDING HART
(Joined 1948. Classification: Law, Tax Attorney)

The son of a prominent attorney and law professor, Stephen Hart came from a family whose history was deeply rooted in pioneer Colorado. Hart was an aggressive businessman who believed in "total client service," handling several hefty cases early in his career, including tax litigation for the estate of *Denver Post* magnate Fred Bonfils. After

founding the law firm Holland and Hart with his friend Josiah G. Holland, he numbered among his clients Claude Boettcher and the Ideal Cement Company. A volunteer for every governor from Ralph Carr to Richard Lamm, he spent two years in the Colorado House of Representatives and four years in the Colorado Senate (1939–1943). Elected to the Board of the Colorado Historical Society in 1938, he engineered passage of the first comprehensive law requiring preservation of public records and archives of historical value. As president of the Society Board from 1959 to 1969, he guided the organization through acquisition of regional museums, including the Grant Humphreys mansion and the Byers-Evans house, and development of Georgetown Historic Mining and Railroad District. A tireless fundraiser, his efforts helped to build the first Colorado History Museum and the Georgetown Loop. After Governor Love made him Colorado's first State Historic Preservation Officer in 1967 (pro bono, since the position was not funded at the time) his most famous battle took place with the Denver Urban Renewal Authority over the D&F Tower, which is still standing because of Hart. The History Colorado Center Library bears his name, as does its annual awards for best historic preservation projects.

In 1979, (left to right) Jim Warner, Governor Dick Lamm, and Stu Moore gathered in the governor's office as he proclaimed Rotary Day. Photo courtesy Denver Rotary Club.

ELREY B. JEPPESEN
(Joined 1962. Classification: Publishing Flying Manuals)

An aviation pioneer whose sixteen-foot bronze statue in leather pilot's helmet, goggles and jodhpurs greets visitors to Denver International Airport, "Jepp" Jeppesen took his first solo flight in 1923 and proudly held one of the first pilot's licenses, which was signed by Orville Wright. A graduate of the University of Denver, as a youngster Jeppesen dropped out of high school to go barnstorming with Tex Rankin's Flying Circus in Portland, Oregon. Jeppesen flew photographic missions for various companies during the 1930s, and as the Depression lifted flew mail in his own Boeing 40B.

In the early days of flight, navigation was so primitive that pilots used road maps to navigate. Jeppesen bought a palm-sized loose-leaf note book to keep records of landmarks, pastures for emergency landings, elevations of obstructions and approaches to airports, designing procedures to be used when visibility was poor. The first to develop flying charts, he decided to print copies and sell the manuals for $10 each. In 1941, he moved to Denver to rent office space for his growing business and continued to fly for United Airlines until 1954. During World War II, the Navy adopted Jepp charts, and after the war commercial airlines contracted for his charts and manuals. Although he sold the firm in 1961, Jeppesen Sanderson (currently part of Boeing) still sells flight information and navigation manuals worldwide. A grateful aviation industry named the main terminal at Denver International Airport in his honor.

Aviation pioneer and Rotarian Elrey P. Jeppesen created charts and manuals that made flying safer for pilots. He moved to Denver in 1941 and rented office space for his expanding manual business, but continued to fly for United Airlines until 1954. The main terminal at Denver International Airport is named in his honor. Photo courtesy George Lundeen.

ROTARY WELCOMED A VARIETY OF GUESTS WITH WIDELY DIVERGENT OPINIONS.

Acclaimed filmmaker Ken Burns (left) chats with producer Stephen Ives. September 5, 1996. Photo courtesy Denver Rotary Club.

Greeley-born Bill Daniels, American cable television pioneer, spoke to the club about the future of cable TV. Photo courtesy Denver Rotary Club.

Alexander Haig, decorated U.S. Army general, served as secretary of state under President Ronald Reagan and White House chief of staff under Presidents Richard Nixon and Gerald Ford. Rotarian Bob Kapelke and University Clubber Jim Cunningham wrote a special song for the 1982 Twelfth Night celebration at the University Club, sung to the tune of Feniculi, Fenicula: "Nuke 'em, nuke 'em, nuke 'em, till they glow! Belt 'em, melt 'em, exfoliate the foe! We can increase the chance of peace if we just go to war today!" Understandably, Haig was not invited to the performance.

Richard E. Fleming, president and CEO of Downtown Denver, Inc., was a force of nature in 1981. Photo courtesy Denver Rotary Club.

Gary Hart, liberal politician, lawyer, author, professor, and commentator who served as a Colorado Democratic senator from 1975 to 1987, and ran in the U.S. presidential elections in 1984 and 1988. Someone wrote him a song too.

A NEW DOWNTOWN DENVER

In 1958, the City and County of Denver established the Denver Urban Renewal Authority, charged with the creation of a "new" Denver. One of their major projects, along with demolition of landmarks like the original Tabor Center and Daniels and Fisher Department Store would be the creation of the Auraria Higher Education Center on the site of the oldest settlement in Denver.

Several Rotarians would be involved in the Auraria project, which involved relocating an entire Hispanic neighborhood across town to make room for the 127-acre urban commuter campus. Movers and shakers included Shelby F. Harper, Denver Rotary president, 1963–64, and chair of the Colorado Commission on Higher Education. Another key figure, Denver University Chancellor and Denver Rotary President Chester M. Alter, 1958–59, has been credited with the suggestion that Community College of Denver, Metropolitan State College of Denver, and the University of Colorado at Denver all share building space and facilities on one campus, a decision that created complications that still exist. Other Rotarians involved included Ray Jenkins, chair of the Downtown Denver Master Plan Committee; Philip Milstein, head of the Downtown Denver Development Committee; Richard W. Wright,

The old Tivoli Brewery, where Denver businessmen occasionally took an afternoon break in the days before the 1965 flood. Tivoli became the Auraria Student Union in the 1990s. Auraria is the largest campus in Colorado, home to Community College of Denver, Metropolitan State College of Denver, and the University of Colorado Denver. Photo courtesy Auraria Higher Education Center.

The Cooper Building at Seventeenth and Curtis Streets became a casualty of the Urban Renewal Authority in 1970. Photo courtesy Denver Public Library Western History Department.

At the August 1976 Rotary Picnic at Elitch Gardens, club members were asked to dress in 1776 or 1876 garb to celebrate the national bicentennial and state centennial. Winners of the costume contest included Andy Pfeiffenberger (left), girl unknown, Jim White (picnic committee chair), Temple "Sandy" Buell, Jim Clayton, James Willard, and Sam Clayton. Photo courtesy Denver Rotary Club.

On January 2, 1975, Rotarians were treated to a presentation on the Auraria project by Richard Wright, former Rotary president, 1959–60; Rotarian Floyd K. Sterns, chair of the Auraria Board; and Judy Fitzgerald, Metro State College student and mother of four. All were optimistic about the prospects for the downtown campus, which would help to accommodate baby boomers entering college.

Despite multiple problems and protests, all three schools were open for business in January 1977 with a combined headcount of more than twenty-six thousand students. Today, Auraria serves 20 percent of all Colorado students in higher education.

As Denver's blossoming preservation community began to feel the far-reaching effects of urban renewal back in 1967, the Denver Landmark Preservation Ordinance made the first attempts to save the city's historic structures. After losing the David Moffat mansion, Historic Denver, Inc., formed in 1970 to successfully rescue the Denver home of Titanic survivor Margaret (Molly) Brown on 1340 Pennsylvania Street.

On May 1, 1975, Barbara Sudler, executive director of Historic Denver, Inc. (future Rotarian), and Ann Love (wife of Rotarian/Governor John Love) spoke to the club about the young organization, whose latest project was Ninth Street Historic Park on the future Auraria Campus. Rescuing an entire block of Victorian houses had turned into a million-dollar project, Sudler reported. She assured the club that Historic Denver, Inc., relied strongly on volunteers and had adopted a "pay as you go" plan with no deficit financing. Interestingly, one of the houses on the block had belonged to Stephen Knight, scion of an entire family of Rotarians.

As the decade faded and 1980s loomed on the horizon, Rotarians could hardly imagine the changes that the next ten years would bring: innovative, far-reaching projects like Artists of America, which would allow Denver Rotary to expand its programs internationally, and a radically altered club that accepted women as full-fledged Rotarians.

It would be a time to remember.

Rotarians pause during a softball game before a picnic at Elitch's in the late 1960s. Top row left: Mark Smith, Pete Thebus, Bill Caile, Preston Smith, Zane Smith, Mike Barrett, Andy Pfeiffenberger, Dick Chisholm, Ernie Seidlitz, Gordon Smith, and others unknown. Second row, seated: unknown, Lew Peevy, Dick Koeppe, Allison Smith, Jim Warner, and others unknown. Photo courtesy Denver Rotary Club.

Past presidents Jim Baxter and Dick Metcalfe (far left and far right) plan the 1985 summer picnic with Stu Moore (center). Photo courtesy Denver Rotary Club.

GOOD TIMES!

At a Fellowship Meeting in April 2010, longtime Rotarians reminisced about the Summer Picnics at the old Elitch Gardens on West Thirty-eighth Avenue and Tennyson Street. F. Tupper Smith, Jr. (joined 1953), former vice president, recalled that some of the members would play softball before the picnic in the parking lot across from Elitch's. The group always met before the game at [Pomponio's] DX because one of the officials was related to the owner.

"The picnic was always in August," said Pete Thebus. "We'd take over the whole park—twelve hundred or more would come. People brought in truckloads of gifts [for the raffle], nice things like TV sets and sporting goods. It was practically a competition to see who could provide the best prizes."

Jim White, who was picnic chair for several years, noted that Temple Buell always donated a case of imported Chivas Regal, which would be distributed by the bottle. "We called out the donor's name each time we gave away a prize, and I guess he liked to hear the sound of his name. One summer, the whole case disappeared. I never did find out what happened to it." (Thebus confessed that he had "accidentally" left the case under one of the tables and later shared the goodies with the Picnic Committee.)

The next year Buell personally brought in two cases. "I had to call out his name twenty-four times," White laughed.

Preston Smith, Jim Clayton, Claud Dutro, and Dan Crippen (left to right) enjoy a summer Rotary Club picnic in 1985. Photo courtesy Denver Rotary Club.

Rotary Club President Jim Warner (1979–1980) horsing around. Dwight Sales sits to the left. (The real story: Club members presented "Geraldine" to Warner while he was club secretary, so that he would have everyone's attention when he made announcements.) Photo courtesy Denver Rotary Club.

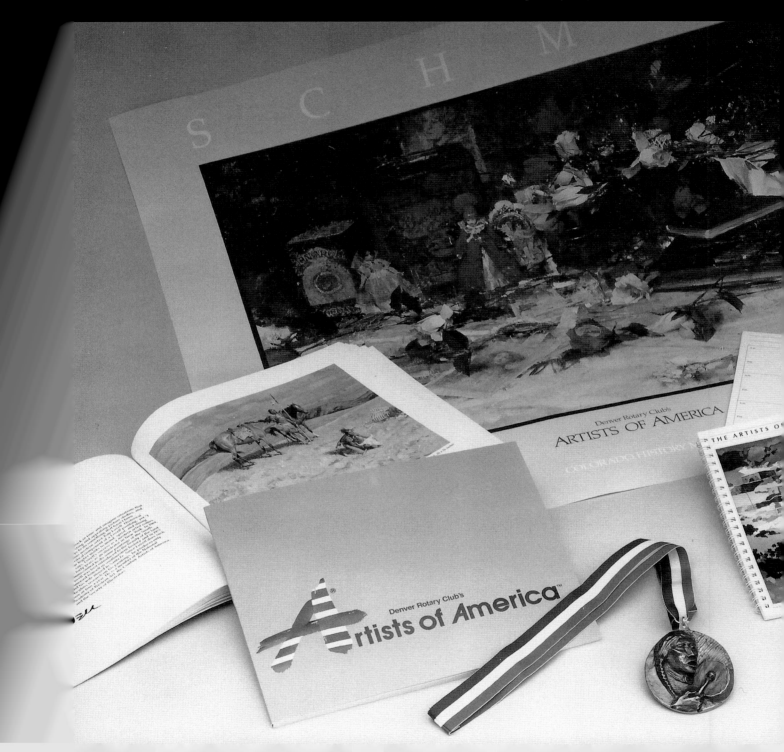

Now and then it's good to pause in our pursuit of happiness and just be happy.

—*Mile High Keyway*, November 10, 1989

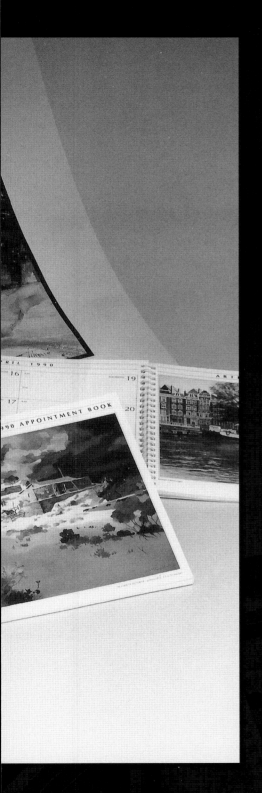

CHAPTER VI

The Revolutionary Years
1980–1990

In 1980, Denverites were still riding the last wave of prosperity from the post–World War II population tsunami. The oil industry boomed, jobs were plentiful, the housing market flourished, and developers got rich as the baby boomers multiplied, the more affluent scuttling off to suburbia with their offspring. Small communities sprang up in areas formerly the domain of prairie dogs and grasshoppers, spawning development in Highlands Ranch, Grant Ranch, Southglenn, and what would eventually become Centennial. Thanks to the 1974 Poundstone Amendment, which froze Denver's boundaries, the city had been spared the burden of supplying water or electricity to these upstarts, but all that tax revenue also remained out of reach. While older towns like Arvada, Aurora, and Lakewood experienced a renaissance of new growth, Denver, like many larger cities around the country, fell victim to inner-city decay.

Stu Moore served as executive director of Denver Rotary for eleven years from 1977 to 1988. He has been an honorary member of the club since August 18, 1977. Photo courtesy Denver Rotary Club.

Commerce also decentralized, which led to some reduction of downtown control over the business community, particularly after George Mackenzie Wallace created the Denver Tech Center, an office megaplex in Greenwood Village. New Rotary clubs formed, including Denver Southeast and Highlands Ranch in 1985, Cherry Creek in 1987, and Mile High in 1989. Most local corporate and nonprofit CEOs still belonged to Denver Rotary, however, or made sure their top executives were members.

"It was a different era," recalls former executive director J. Stuart (Stu) Moore, 1977–1988. "Corporate offices and banks were locally owned or managed. I could walk into any corporation or bank in town, even without an appointment, and the CEO or president would see me."

Although oil never gushed from the ground in these parts, the city's petroleum tycoons still reigned, making multimillionaires out of John and Kenneth King (no relationship), Marvin Davis, Cortland Dietler, Frederick Mayer, Fred Hamilton, Jerome Lewis, and Phil Anschutz. When the oil boom fizzled in the mid-1980s, followed by significant layoffs by high-tech companies, the domino effect led to failure of several large industrial banks. The most infamous was Silverado, which the federal government eventually took over to the tune of nearly $2 billion. Many people lost homes and savings in the recession, which would not be dwarfed until 2007–09.

Denver businesses remained relatively stable in the 1980s and the city still looked pretty good to outsiders, with a glistening skyline barely recognizable from the 1950s. Shoveling away downtown's rubble, developers planted a new crop of office buildings, which popped out of the ground like dandelions in a field of concrete. New additions during the early 1980s included the fifty-six-story Republic Plaza, the fifty-four-story City Center Tower, and the fifty-two-story United Bank Tower, lovingly nicknamed the "Cash Register Building." Ironically, the individual most responsible for demolishing many of Denver's grand old buildings (J. Robert Cameron, director of Denver Urban Renewal Authority) and the woman who campaigned vigorously to rescue what remained (Barbara Sudler, director of Historic Denver) both belonged to Denver Rotary. After all, it was a pretty big club, with 607 members by June 1989.

"Rotary was never about politics," said Stu Moore. "It was always about business, about promoting Denver and giving back to the community. Everything else, even personal friendship, was secondary."

On November 10, 1988, guest speakers Denver Mayor Federico Peña and Rotarian Richard L. Deane (1966), chair of the Denver Planning Board, spoke at a luncheon meeting about a new "Comprehensive Plan for Denver," scheduled for public hearings early in 1989. The plan, according to *Mile High Keyway*, focused on regional cooperation between Denver and its suburban neighbors "instead of competition and feuding," and efforts to make Denver a more "livable" city.

Mayor Peña addressed questions about the new airport, scheduled to begin construction in 1989. A young lawyer who became Denver's first Hispanic mayor, Peña won the election of 1984 with the slogan, "Imagine a Great City." His campaign had benefited greatly from the fortuitous Christmas Eve blizzard of 1982, which shed some light (and heat) on the deficiencies in Mayor Bill McNichols' snow removal plan.

Despite the recession, Peña pushed for progress, including a new convention center and super-airport, which he promised would move Denver into the big leagues as a convention and tourism target. His talk reiterated the theme that a new airport would be critical for Denver to compete in a "global economy," a new phrase being bandied about to describe a world that was shrinking even in the days before the Internet. Like Stapleton Airport in 1929, the Denver International Airport project would be riddled with controversy, charges of corruption, land swindles, and a budget that skyrocketed above original estimates. After President Clinton recruited Peña as his secretary of transportation, many of the glitches would fall into the lap of his successor, Wellington Webb. When DIA finally opened in 1995, however, it fulfilled its promise to keep Denver competitive in the air age, becoming one of the country's busiest, largest, and most efficient airports.

"ARTISTS OF AMERICA" PAINTS THE TOWN

At the annual trustees meeting on July 8, 1980, the ambitious Denver Rotary Club Foundation set a fundraising goal of $1 million by the club's seventy-fifth anniversary in 1986. In search of a fundraiser that would net more than the modest $150,000 currently in the till, Grant Wilkins and the foundation's new president, H. Preston Smith, along with other members of the committee, came up with a new plan.

"I had just gotten into the early phase of art collection," Wilkins recalled. "To learn more, my wife and I went to national shows, like the Cowboy Artists of America in Phoenix and the National Academy of Western Art (now called the "Prix de West") at the Cowboy Hall of Fame in Oklahoma City. At these shows, which are still going on, by the way, we met some of the leading artists in the country.

Wildlife sculptress Sherry Salari Sander and her impressive equine sculpture made a hit at the AOA show. Photo courtesy Denver Rotary Club.

About the same time, we bought a townhouse in Santa Fe, which is the number two art center in the U.S. We spent a lot of our spare time learning more about art, particularly American Indian art, and about Taos founders, who are now as famous and expensive as Remington and Russell."

About the same time, Carolyn and Preston Smith attended an art show while vacationing in California. Before long, Wilkins and the Smiths were discussing the possibility of an art show as a Denver Rotary Foundation fundraiser. "Grant had lots of contacts

Artists visit Preston and Carolyn Smith's ranch in 1980. Front row, standing left to right, artist Jim Kramer, Jim K. Fritty, Chen Zu Min (wife of Chen Chi), Chen Chi, Tom Jones, and Glenna Goodacre. Back row: Preston Smith and Julie Smith on the horse. The Great Dane, Buddy, belonged to the Smiths. Photo courtesy Denver Rotary Club.

Governor Richard D. Lamm poses for portrait artist E. R. Kintsler. Photo courtesy Denver Rotary Club.

that would be crucial to the future of Artists of America," Carolyn Smith said.

They first set up a meeting with a small group of popular Santa Fe artists. Governor Richard D. Lamm, an honorary Rotarian like all Denver mayors and Colorado governors, saw the prospective show as an opportunity to promote Denver in the art world and draw attention away from the state's less than stellar economy.

"Dick Lamm was excited about the project and wanted to host all the artists at the governor's mansion the night before the show," said Wilkins, who chaired the first AOA committee. "He even flew the Foundation committee to Oklahoma City and Santa Fe in the state plane."

"We heard that Oklahoma City might want to move their show to Denver, so we went there first," said Stu Moore, who remembers hitting his head on the plane's ceiling during a particularly bumpy ride over Kansas. Apparently news of Denver's interest caught the attention of the press and rallied Oklahoma City art lovers, which Smith and Moore suspect may have been that city's goal all along. At any rate, that particular show stayed in the "Sooner State."

In Santa Fe, the committee met with top artists Wilson Hurley, Bettina Steinke, Clark Hulings, Glenna Goodacre, and portrait artist Everett Raymond Kintsler. "We told the artists that we wanted to do a show similar to those in Phoenix and Oklahoma City," Wilkins said. "But we wanted to make ours better. When we asked them for ideas, they suggested 1) making the show about American artists, not just Western art, and 2) doing away with the practice of jurying artists. To make the show more prestigious, we should ask only artists who had 'arrived.' They would want to look good among their peers and give us their best work."

Taking their advice, the committee began preparing for the exhibition, scheduled on September 11, 1981, at the Colorado Heritage Center at 1300 Broadway, which later became the Colorado History Museum. After the preview exhibition and sale, the artwork would be displayed at the museum for the next month.

During the interim, Wilson Hurley made several trips to meet with the Planning Committee in Denver. In a presentation to Rotarians on March 11, he stressed the importance of the sale as impetus for a resurgence of interest in true American art like the Hudson River School (i.e., Albert Bierstadt, Thomas Moran), not just American artists who copied the style of European painters. After Hurley's talk, the Denver Rotary Club Foundation requested 150 volunteers for the AOA debut, which would host sixty-six artists, 159 paintings, $2.5 million worth of art, and bring in more than a thousand guests.

Guests sign in for an AOA reception at the governor's mansion. Back, Jane and John Andrews. Marlene Wilkins is looking through nametags at the table. Photo courtesy Denver Rotary Club.

"Our show became a favorite among the artists," said Wilkins, "probably because we treated them royally. Instead of sloppy joes in the garden like Oklahoma City, we held cocktail parties at the governor's mansion, followed by a sit-down dinner at the Hilton or some other good hotel."

Typically, one Rotarian would be assigned to entertain each artist and handle the sales on the opening night. For the entire weekend, the artist would stay with the host, who would introduce him or her to other Rotarians. In later years, the club paid for hotel rooms and most meals.

AOA was a fixed price sale, not an auction. People put their names in a box and at 8:30 p.m. a drawing would be held and the winner announced. Not everyone claimed the prize, however.

"Some individuals would bid on several pieces of art, more than they could afford, so they had to pick what they really wanted," said Wilkins. "If they didn't show up, another name would be drawn. And, of course, others bought all they bid on, like Phil Anchutz, who came to the first show. A lot of people had told us that Denver's a lousy art town and nobody makes any money here, but that first night we sold nearly half a million dollars worth of art."

Over the next few years, the show continued to gain prestige, generating $5 million in sales by 1985. The artists kept approximately 70 to 75 percent of the profit from the sale, the Colorado History Museum earned a percentage and the remainder after expenses went to the Denver Rotary Club Foundation, which reported in its 1990 catalog that, "Proceeds from nearly $1.5 million have been distributed to fund and support youth-oriented programs and educational opportunities in our community." According to Executive Director Darlene Mast, during its twenty-year history, AOA generated art sales totaling $14 million, with $1,894,032 going to the Denver Rotary Club Foundation and $803,467 to the Colorado Historical Society.

Bill and Phyllis Beattie chat with Stu Moore (center) during an AOA dinner. Photo courtesy Denver Rotary Club.

"AOA became one of the most important art shows in the country," Smith observed. "Although Rotarians formed the nucleus of patrons, this was a major social event with a lot of hands on participation, one of the highlights of the year.

"The show was a real learning adventure, not just a matter of seeing art," she added. "The Colorado History Museum sponsored related programs and activities, and some of us became docents and took children on tours. School buses from all over the state brought students to the museum."

AOA also provided an opportunity for members to form lasting friendships with some of the artists. "One year my husband picked up Chen Chi at the airport, a remarkable artist who became a good friend," Smith recalled. "We stayed in touch for many years."

Another program soon emerged from AOA, the Santa Fe Weekend. Executive Director Stu Moore would make arrangements for the annual event, during which different artists each year would host a party at their homes for visiting Denver Rotarians. "We had one every year, usually in mid-summer," said Moore. "Like the show, it was a lot of work to make all the arrangements, but everybody had a good time."

"The artists were very grateful to us, and they entertained us lavishly," Smith recalled. "One year, Allan Houser even redecorated his patio and brought in Native American dancers to entertain us."

Rotarian Richard Gooding and Chen Chi pose next to one of the artist's paintings. Photo courtesy Denver Rotary Club.

ROTARY MOVES TO ERADICATE POLIO

The success of AOA allowed the Denver Rotary Club Foundation to move to the next level. On February 23, 1985, as Rotary International celebrated eighty years of community service, Rotarians worldwide were conducting large-scale health care, nutrition, and community development projects around the globe through the RI Foundation's Health, Hunger, and Humanities Program. At the time, approximately 150 Denver Rotarians had contributed more than $150,000 to RI Foundation projects, including an expanding polio immunization campaign that had already reached eight countries. In July 1986, RI led a worldwide fund-raising program to raise $120 million with the goal of immunizing people in all nations of the western hemisphere by 1990.

In October 1987, Denver Rotary began a campaign to raise $500,000 for the cause. The club got behind campaign leader Dick Reuss, particularly after the Colorado Trust awarded the club a $100,000 challenge grant. Club President Dave Fleming, 1987–88, inoculated his granddaughter at one of the meetings.

By April 13, 1988, Denver Rotary had $526,902, the largest amount ever raised for a single project and the most contributed to PolioPlus by any Rotary Club in the United States.

One driving force behind this astonishing achievement, Grant Wilkins, has been called "the quintessential Rotarian." A former Denver Rotary president and RI director, Wilkins was a polio survivor. He contracted the disease in 1951 while on a business trip to Kansas and spent six painful weeks in the hospital, at one point undergoing a new procedure called a tracheotomy. During his recovery, his wife Diane developed a different strain of polio. She spent the next two and a half years in the hospital in a chest respirator, paralyzed from the neck down.

"Diane was a remarkable person," Wilkins wrote in a 1995 article for *The Rotarian*. "She maintained a calm, spiritual outlook that was an inspiration to everyone, including myself. We tried to lead as normal a life as possible, given the severity of her condition. . . . She continued to be a wonderful mother, talking with the children and even helping them with their homework. She carried on the best she could for thirteen years, when she died from kidney failure."

Wilkins' personal tragedy motivated him to become a major proponent of PolioPlus and a member of the U.S.C.B. (United States, Canada, and Bermuda) PolioPlus Committee. In 1986, he asked sculptor Glenna Goodacre, one of the original Santa Fe artists in AOA, to create a symbol for the PolioPlus Program.

AOA Chair Grant Wilkins presents DRCF President Preston Smith with a $150,000 check for the Denver Rotary Club Foundation while DRC President Pete Smythe applauds in the foreground. Photo courtesy Denver Rotary Club.

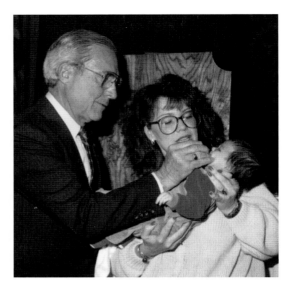

The gifted sculptor, creator of the Vietnam Women's Memorial, later recalled that the "little project" she had originally envisioned became a consuming enterprise for the next nine years.

Goodacre's original design depicted a Rotarian seated on a bench, giving drops of polio vaccine to a baby as two older children of different ethnic backgrounds watch at his knee. Miniature statuettes were given to major donors. In 1990, Rotary International leaders commissioned her to create a seven-foot bronze statue to stand in front of the Rotary International offices at One Rotary Center in Evanston, Illinois. The artist has since created three more bronze statues. The second, dedicated April 6, 1995, pictures a Rotarian administering oral vaccine to a baby. Located on the Sixteenth Street Mall for many years, it has since been transferred to Anschutz Medical Campus. The others have been installed in Denton, Texas, and Omaha, Nebraska.

At a kickoff meeting for PolioPlus on October 22, 1987, Club President Dave Fleming and his daughter Shelley Fleming Black administer the polio vaccine to his grandson Devin. The act symbolized the Denver Rotary Club's commitment to raise $500,000 for PolioPlus, double the share set for them by Rotary International. Photo courtesy Denver Rotary.

Artist Glenna Goodacre sculpted the PolioPlus statue at Grant Wilkins' request. Photo courtesy Denver Rotary Club.

Mayor Wellington Webb officiates at the dedication of the PolioPlus statue on the Sixteenth Street Mall in 1995. Left to right: Tom Rogers, DDI Director Bill Mosher, 1995–96 RI President Herbert Brown, Richard Gooding, Mayor Webb, and sculptor Glenna Goodacre. Photo courtesy Denver Rotary Club.

COMMITTEES, PROGRAMS, AND ACTIVITIES

During the 1980s, Denver Rotarians could choose to serve on any one of nearly forty committees, in areas including Athletic/Sports, Youth Services, International Service, Budget, District Conference, Membership, Historical, Inner-City Conferences, Artists of America, and PolioPlus.

For such a large club, Denver Rotary funds were managed efficiently. An operating budget of $412,000 in 1988–89 allowed $339,800 for cash expenses (administrative, meals, salaries, etc.), $36,000 for organizational expenses (RI dues, district conference, regional meetings), and $36,300 for committee expenses, including the three major social events, the Picnic ($7,500), Sweetheart Ball ($14,000), and the Family Holiday Party ($11,000).

Youth Mentoring Program

By June 1985, sixty-nine students were benefiting from Denver Rotary's new mentoring program aimed at gifted children. Youngsters from nineteen Denver Public schools worked with volunteer mentors from Rotary in areas of mutual interest, ranging from French and sketching to aerospace and DNA research. One fourth-grader worked with an architect to design a home of the future, learning about site construction, landscaping, materials, and design. Another group from Cole Middle School entered the Olympics of the Mind competition, finishing second in the state. Community Resources, Inc., which worked with Denver schools to provide enrichment opportunities, managed the program, which was funded by Denver Rotary Foundation, the Denver and Frost Foundations, Mobil Oil, and Rockwell International.

Rotary Home Exchange

This program, which began in 1975, became extremely popular during the 1980s. Rotarians worldwide had the opportunity to vacation in another country (or their own country) with their families and actually become involved in the daily lives of other Rotarians. An international Home Exchange Directory listed the member, contact number, areas of interest, time of year, number of members in the family, length of stay, and other pertinent information. All arrangements would be made between members, and the decision to exchange was strictly personal.

Fellowship Meetings

Since Denver Rotary membership had become so large, Executive Director Stu Moore and Preston Smith, president in 1977–78, initiated a new program called Fellowship Meetings, in which small groups of about fifteen members would meet at the offices of other Denver Rotarians.

"We would have a list of host members, and each Rotarian would sign up to let us know where he wanted to go," said Moore, who made the arrangements. Fellowship Meetings have been held quarterly ever since, with about fifteen members visiting each location.

These small gatherings, mixing social and business chit-chat, have become a Denver Rotary tradition, giving members a chance to get to know each other on a more personal basis.

SAY GOODBYE TO THE COSMO

This photo was taken in 1982, two years before the Cosmo came down in a rain of brick and ashes. This is a view of the older section (originally the Metropole Hotel, circa 1891) and the popular Polynesian restaurant, Don the Beachcomber. Photo courtesy Denver Public Library Western History Department.

In May 1984, the Cosmopolitan Hotel joined the Albany, the Shirley Savoy, and the Windsor as another casualty of Denver's demolition derby. Since TV's *Alfred Hitchcock Show* used the Cosmo's collapse in one of the episodes, at this writing, images of the implosion can be viewed online.

"Our offices had been in the Cosmo for years and naturally we didn't want to move," said Stu Moore. "As I recall, some Canadian company was going to put up an office building. Nothing ever happened, and unfortunately it's still a parking lot."

Oddly, *Mile High Keyway* never mentions the impending change in venue, nor did there seem to be much sentiment attached to the old homestead (or the Albany Hotel, which fell to the wrecking ball in 1977) despite Denver Rotary's longtime connections. The last meeting at the Cosmo took place December 16, 1982. That year, the Holiday Party was held at the Denver Hilton, reincarnated in 2010 as the Sheraton Denver Downtown Hotel. Afterward, Rotary gatherings were held at the Denver Athletic Club at Thirteenth and Glenarm Streets, where most meetings and larger parties have been held ever since. Among the most prestigious private clubs in the country, the DAC was founded in 1884 so that those "engaged in indoor pursuits might gain healthful diversion."

"For awhile we looked at various hotels like, the Hilton and the Fairmont [now Marquis-Fairmont] before settling on the Denver Athletic Club for meetings," Moore added. "At first they didn't want us, thought they couldn't accommodate so large a group, but it all worked out."

DENVER ROTARY ALLOWS WOMEN TO JOIN THE CLUB

Women's admission to Rotary came after a long struggle that began just a few years after Paul Harris formed the first Rotary Club in 1905. Naturally a few women protested their exclusion, like the Women's Rotary of Minneapolis, which formed as a stand-alone club in 1912. Few complained, however, since women still could not vote in most states. Colorado was actually the first state where men voted to enfranchise women in 1893.

Most women simply supported Rotary through their husbands, an arrangement that neatly excluded unmarried women. In 1921, Rotarian wives formed the Ladies of the Rotary, often called the Rotary Anns, but the women's groups were never formally recognized by Rotary International. Despite the advent of the women's movement in the late 1960s and 1970s, RI steadfastly voted down any attempts to allow women membership.

The first serious challenge to the men-only imperative came in 1977. In celebration of their twenty-fifth anniversary, the Rotary Club of Duarte, a small town in Los Angeles County, voted to add three women members. Naturally, RI terminated the club's charter. Undaunted, the Duarte Club filed a lawsuit against RI's decision, but in 1983, the California Superior Court ruled in RI's favor. Three years later, the Court of Appeals reversed the decision. When the California Supreme Court refused to hear the case, it went to the U.S. Supreme Court. Finally, on May 4, 1987, the Court ruled that Rotary Clubs could not exclude women from membership based on gender alone. Subsequently, RI issued a policy statement allowing any Rotary Club in the United States to admit qualified women into membership.

Hidehiko Iwasaki of Matsumaya Rotary Club poses with President Jean Jones, 1995–96, one of the first women to join Denver Rotary and the first female club president. Photo courtesy Denver Rotary Club.

"After the Supreme Court decision, I got several calls from newspapers asking how Denver Rotary was going to handle it," said Stu Moore. "At the time I wasn't quite sure myself, but it's turned out to be a very good thing. About twenty or thirty members quit the club when we admitted women, not that bad out of a membership of six hundred."

Three months later, on July 9, 1987, 96 percent of Denver Rotarians voted to admit women who met the requirements of bylaws and constitution. The first four women members would be admitted in September: Rosemary E. Weiss, managing partner, Weiss and Company; Donna L. Dorre, vice president of the American Cancer Society, Colorado Division; Barbara Sudler Hornby, president of the Colorado Historical Society; and Jean C. Jones, director of the Girl Scouts.

Jones, who became Denver Rotary's first woman president in 1995, felt "very comfortable" as one of the first women in the club. "By the time the club decided to take in women, most of the men who didn't want to support it had already resigned," she recalled. "It was easier for me since my grandfather had been a member for a long time and my husband was a member. As CEO of Girl Scouts I had many friends in the club, including a few who were still around from my grandfather's day."

Jones said she immediately got involved with the Rotary Scholarship Fund. "I worked hard. As one of the first women, I felt a special obligation to join in committees, attend all meetings, and take on difficult jobs. Back in 1987, Rotary expected

Denver Broncos/Denver Rotary Scholars are honored at the August 20, 1987 meeting. Left to right, Dave Fleming (club president), Wendell Waggoner (Denver Boys, Inc.), Andrea Cubin, Jodianne Kreutzer, Tamara Lebsock, and Bob Hurley (Denver Broncos). Photo courtesy Denver Rotary Club.

nearly perfect attendance. If you couldn't get to a meeting, you had to make it up." (Even during the 1920s, the Denver newsletter featured a section called "Roaming Rotarians—They Didn't Forget," which recognized members who made up meetings in other towns, states and countries.)

Apparently, breaking the ice wasn't all that difficult. "I remember at one of my early meetings wading my way through the crowd and trying to find a place to sit among a sea of men. The center table was supposed to be reserved for old-timers, but a good friend, Justice Robert McWilliams, brought me over and introduced me to the group, which made me feel like I was really 'in.' Some of the newer male members wondered why I got to sit at the center table and they didn't, and after that the tradition died out.

"Of course, we had to contend with the occasional tasteless joke, but in general we were treated with consideration," she added. "We were fortunate because many European countries still didn't want women members. They got around the rules by forming all-women groups instead."

Carolyn Smith, former development director for the Junior League of Denver, joined on January 2, 1988. She felt welcomed by Denver Rotarians from her first meeting. "Mine was a unique membership because my husband, Preston Smith, had been so active in the club. I knew many of the members and understood the set-up.

"Women appreciated the fact that the men were wary at first, but they finally realized we didn't want to change things. Being one of the first women was a real honor for me."

Students perform at the 1983 Scholastic Arts Award Exhibition. Photo courtesy Denver Rotary Club.

Another pioneer, Lee Harding Everding, was a psychiatric social worker and CEO of Communicom Corporation of America, a holding company for Eastern AM radio stations.

"I remember being very warmly welcomed," she said. "I enjoyed the opportunity to meet and learn from so many leaders, largely men at the time. The CEO after my name opened many doors that an LSW (Licensed Social Worker) might not have."

She first became involved with Rotary through Denver Girls, Inc. "My husband, Dick Kylberg, had been a Rotarian and he suggested that I contact them about sponsoring Denver Girls, since they sponsored Denver Boys. At that time I was the chair of Denver Girls, which began with the Junior League of Denver. The League only supported causes for three years and then passed the project on to another group in the community.

"When I went to Denver Rotary with this idea and request, they took Denver Girls under their wing. Ultimately they merged Denver Girls with Denver Boys and the project became Denver Kids, Inc."

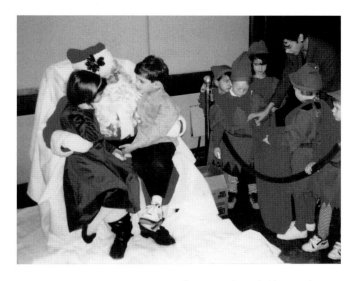

Dressed as mini-elves, children and grandchildren of Rotarians line up to visit Santa. Photo courtesy Denver Rotary Club.

MOVING AHEAD

Denver Rotary took major strides during the 1980s, admitting women to full membership, raising the most funds in history for PolioPlus, initiating the Artists of America program, and broadening Denver Boys and Denver Girls support. During the next decade, the club would continue to expand its influence with programs, projects and accomplishments that founders could never have imagined.

Grant and Jim Wilkins share their wish lists with Santa. His verdict: two nice, zero naughty. Photo courtesy Denver Rotary Club.

Stu Moore, Barbara Sudler Hornby, and Bill Hornby kibitz at a Rotary gathering. Photo courtesy Denver Rotary Club.

My father was eighty-six when he died. As an old man, he was still planting peach and apple trees on our farm near Portsmouth, Ohio. When I asked who would take in the fruit he said, "That's not important. I just want to live every day as if I were going to live forever."

—Branch Rickey

In the 1920s, Rotarian Charles Gates (center, back row) sponsored his own team, the Gates Half Soles. Photo courtesy Denver Public Library Western History Department.

99

CHAPTER VII

Beyond Borders
1991–1999

DENVER IN THE 1990s

The final decade of the millennium heralded another economic boom in Denver, particularly after DIA opened in 1995. Unfortunately, it also signaled the demise of many long-time, locally owned and operated businesses. Certain banks definitely had problems, despite reassurances by Rotary luncheon guest speaker Richard A. Kirk, president of the American Banking Association, on April 19, 1991.

Bank failures during the late 1980s prompted massive liquidations or mergers, beginning in 1988 when First Bank System, Inc. (now U.S. Bancorp) took control of Central Bank of Denver. The subsequent demolition of Central Bank's Beaux Arts classic (designed by Jacques Benedict, 1911) aroused protests, but preservationists found themselves powerless against the ubiquitous wrecking ball. Takeovers continued as Colorado National Bank disappeared into U.S. Bank and, in 1991, Norwest Corporation swallowed up the United Banks of Colorado. The most spectacular changes occurred in 1998, when the Wells Fargo/Norwest Bank conglomerate gained control of the American National Bank of Denver, First National Bank of Denver, Columbia Savings, and several others. Interstate banking had a huge impact as Colorado lost the headquarters of several large banking institutions and the community connectedness that came with those top management people. Some experts maintained that bank customers actually benefited from improved banking products and services while others bemoaned the loss of local control.

Demolition of the historic Central Bank of Denver in the late 1980s sparked a major public protest by preservationists, but the wrecking ball won the day. Photo courtesy Denver Public Library Western History Department.

A free shuttle on the Sixteenth Street Mall, pictured here in 1990, takes riders from RTD Civic Center Park to LoDo. Photo courtesy VISIT DENVER: The Convention and Visitors Bureau.

In response to a changing market, other local businesses would be absorbed by larger companies or disappear completely. The Gates family sold Gates Rubber Company to a British conglomerate in 1996, and Public Service of Colorado became Xcel Energy with headquarters in Minneapolis. Department stores that had been in operation since the 1870s would be swallowed up by bigger fish—Joslin's by Dillards in 1998 and May D&F by Foleys, which Macy's bought out in 2006. In other parts of the state, Charles Boettcher's Ideal Industries melted into the Holnam Corporation. The behemoth Colorado Fuel and Iron Company ceased operations in 1998 and is now owned by Evraz Group SA, a Russian steel corporation. Some administration buildings from the old plant were converted into the Steelworks Museum of Industry and Culture.

For Denver Rotary, the corporate musical chair game meant that many bank presidents and other CEOs now resided out of state. As a result, Rotary widened its parameters, although many Rotarians held the title of president, vice president, partner in a law firm or director of a company, organization, or foundation.

Many longtime local enterprises, now under new management, kept their names, including City Floral and Robinson Dairy. Coors Brewery also retained its identity despite a merger with Molson of Montreal (2005), which crated Molson-Coors. The company joined with SAB Miller in 2008 to create Miller-Coors and flourished despite competition from Anheuser-Bush in Fort Collins. The pair, along with numerous microbreweries, made Colorado the country's number one beer-making state. Other leading industries during the 1990s included aerospace, defense, electronics, communications, and the cable companies.

Geographically and population-wise, Denver grew for the first time since the 1970s. Lowry Air Force Base and Stapleton Airport closed, to be replaced by upscale housing developments, apartment complexes, and shopping areas attempting to capture a small town ambiance. The City and County of Denver's population had increased from 467,601 in 1990 to 554,636 in 2000, and in the first decade of the new millennium, the six-county metro area soared to 2.4 million. The burgeoning population created a traffic nightmare that would finally abate somewhat with the T-REX project at the southern edge of I-25 in the new millennium.

With nineteen accidents and one fatality the first year, Light Rail debuted on October 7, 1994, on a 5.3-mile track that ran from West Colfax on the Auraria Campus to Thirtieth Avenue and Downing Street. As historian Tom Noel jokingly assured Rotarians at the April 27, 1994 luncheon, "The light rail is quiet. Ask anyone who has been hit by it."

A DOWNTOWN RENAISSANCE

The affluent 1990s helped to create a downtown where active younger people wanted to live. In 1983, Historic Denver had moved to Union Station to lead a campaign that would designate Lower Downtown (LoDo) a historic district, attempting a late-hour rescue before demolitionists got a grip on the area between Larimer and Wynkoop Streets from Fourteenth to Twentieth Streets. Formation of the Lower Downtown Historic District in 1988 rescued more than one hundred historic buildings in the city's oldest neighborhood, primarily a warehouse district at the time. LoDo subsequently became a destination neighborhood blossoming with lofts, art galleries, bars, restaurants, entertainment venues, and new businesses, particularly after Coors Field (1993) brought legions of baseball fans downtown.

In October 1994, Denver Rotary and University Hills Rotary sponsored a new club in LoDo. The forming members included Mary Dawson, Breckenridge Grover,

This photo shows the Colorado Convention Center during construction in 1990. Photo courtesy Denver Rotary Club.

Baseball fans including Roger Kinney (bottom row, far right) and Grant Wilkins (top row, second from the right) made a stop at Coors Field with RI directors who were considering Denver as a site for a future RI Convention. Back row, left to right, are Bill Fox, who was meetings division manager of RI; Jack Forrest; Jerry Barden, director RI, 1995–97, and Grant Wilkins. In the stall by himself is Angelo S. Carella, local host chair and committee member of the 1990 Portland, Oregon, Rotary Interntional Convention. The two women in the front row have not been identified. Photo courtesy Denver Rotary Club.

Roy Berkeley, and John Hickenlooper, future mayor and governor, a key figure in the creation of Colorado's microbrewing industry. Meetings were originally held at Hickenlooper's restaurant, the Wynkoop Brewery.

An economy on the upswing meant new civic and cultural projects. On July 15, 1991, new City Librarian Rick Ashton spoke to Rotarians about the forthcoming $91.6 million bond issue for a new main library in Civic Center. Designed by Michael Graves, the colorful five-story structure at Fourteenth and Broadway would prove an excellent staging area for President Bill Clinton's 1997 Summit of Eight, a meeting that brought Denver the most illustrious gathering ever of international heads of state.

In 1988, voters approved the Scientific Cultural Facilities District (SCFD), which allotted one-tenth of 1 percent sales tax to support region's scientific and cultural facilities. Although smaller organizations would profit, the big winners were the Tier I organizations, including the Denver Art Museum, the Denver Performing Arts Center, the Denver Zoo, the Denver Botanic Gardens, and the Denver Museum of Nature and Science. Each would undergo extensive expansion, physically and programmatically, during the next twenty years. In 1993, public relations guru Floyd Ciruli spoke to the club about the cultural benefits reaped by the SCFD, which most Denver Rotarians supported. Voters extended the expiration date until 2004, and subsequently until 2018. The SCFD has become a national model for government funding of cultural organizations.

During the mid- to late 1990s, the city's flirtation with major league sports became a full-fledged love affair. Of course, Denverites had long been football fans. In 1959, thanks to owner/Rotarian Bob Howsam, the Denver Broncos were awarded an American Football League charter franchise. Following an AFL/NFL merger, which Howsam helped to engineer, the team became part of the American Football Conference (AFC) Western Division in the National Football League. After several false starts, their back-to-back Superbowl wins in 1997–98 inspired Denverites to replace the outdated but serviceable Mile High Stadium with Invesco Field at Mile High, which opened in 2001.

Denver's other major league sports teams included the Denver Nuggets (basketball), the Colorado Mammoths (lacrosse), and the Colorado Avalanche (ice hockey), which rumbled in from Quebec to win the Stanley Cup in 1996 and 2001. The $180 million Pepsi Center was constructed as part of a downtown sports arena expansion that included Invesco Field and Coors Field. By the next decade, Colorado's major league soccer team, the Colorado Rapids, also had a new super-stadium at Dick's Sporting Goods Park in Commerce City. Denver would have more professional sports teams than any other city in the country.

While Denver Rotary supported all local sports, Major League Baseball would have the most impact on the club and its programs.

DENVER ROTARY AND THE COLORADO ROCKIES

Denver's baseball history goes back to 1862, when Rocky Mountain News owner William Newton Byers published the following notice:

All those wishing to join a base ball club to play according to the rules of modern or New York games will meet this evening at Whipple's Cabinet Shop . . . to effect a permanent organization.

The newly formed Colorado Baseball Club played their first game that year at the Broadway Grounds on Colfax and Broadway, near the present site of the RTD Civic Center station. The field hosted various amateur and semi-pro teams until 1885, when the city secured its first all-salaried team. The following year, the Denvers won the first Western League pennant at a new field on Thirty-second and Market Streets.

Denver Pavilions debuted in 1998, bringing suburbanites and tourists back to the city. Photo courtesy VISIT DENVER: The Convention and Visitors Bureau.

In 1900, star player George Tebeau, cofounder of the American League, won a minor league franchise for Denver and the team became the Denver Bears. For many years, professional games were held at Merchants Park on Exposition and South Broadway. In 1947 the Howsam family bought the Bears and built Bears stadium on site of the old city dump near Federal Boulevard and Ninetenth Avenue. The Howsams remodeled the playing field and renamed it Mile High Stadium in 1968. Eventually, Gerald and Alan Phipps bought the team from the Howsams and, under the leadership of Jim Burris, the Bears prospered for many years. After real estate entrepreneur John Dikeou bought the team in 1984, they became the Denver Zephyrs.

Rotarians Roger Kinney and Barbara Sudler Hornby preside at an awards banquet. Kinney has been credited as the man who brought baseball to Denver; Hornby became one of the first four women Rotarians and the first woman president of the Colorado Historical Society. Photo courtesy Denver Rotary Club.

"Denver Rotary has always been very supportive of baseball," said Rotarian Roger Kinney, who recalls an early photo of Rotarians seated around a radio during a luncheon, listening to a broadcast of the World Series. "Unfortunately, early efforts to bring the major leagues to Denver [initiated by Rotarian Bob Howsam and supported by fellow club members Bick Bluestein, Hoyt Brawner, and John Andrews] were never successful. But in the late 1980s, when the National League decided to expand by two teams, the Colorado State Legislature passed a bill that created a Metropolitan Stadium District and a Colorado Baseball Commission."

A longtime supporter of city and local sports, Kinney (who brought the NCAA Final Four basketball tournament to Denver in 1989) would be appointed by Governor Roy Romer to the Metropolitan Stadium Authority. Together with Denver Rotarians Carroll Speckman and Joe Blake, he helped to stage a spectacular

The Rotary Club Board of Directors gather before the Stock Show. Back row, left to right: Gary Armstrong, Dennis Graham, Dan Crippen, Tom Rogers, Marie Canfield (executive director), Jim Wilkins, and Bill Houston. Front row, left to right: John Lucken, Mike O'Connell, Carol Hamil Henderson, Jack Barker, Jean Stewart, and Scott Steinhauer.

rally in the atrium of the United Bank Center for the benefit of the visiting delegation from the National League.

In 1990, Kinney became the director of the Colorado Baseball Commission, charged with creating a campaign for a passage of a bond issue to build the new baseball complex. He recalled that Rotarian support helped to win the day. "When we were successful with the vote to get the new stadium (August 14, 1990), we ran into trouble when the Dikeou family [real estate developers] decided not to be owners," he said. "As it turned out, the price for the team was substantially higher than anyone expected, nearly $100 million. We were left without a strong owner, and Major League Baseball insisted on local ownership.

"Dick Anderson, a great Rotarian and baseball fan [later director of Stapleton Development] made arrangements for Governor Roy Romer to meet with Jim Baldwin, Dick Robinson, and a few others, who later served on a Search Committee for the first ownership group. It was controversial at the time, but it moved the process forward, and time was important. Once Pete Coors, Jerry McMorris, and the Monfort family became involved, we were on our way. As I look back on it, if Anderson and Baldwin had not involved the governor, we might not have succeeded."

After the franchise was awarded on July 5, 1991, the Colorado Rockies held a banquet at the Denver Marriott City Center to welcome Major League Baseball to Denver and recognize volunteers. "A committee of Rotarians, chaired by Jim Wilkins, helped to organize the event," recalled Kinney, who became the Rockies' community relations director and their first employee. "Fay Vincent, commissioner of Major League Baseball; Bill White, president of the National League; Seymor Simmons, president of Denver Rotary; and Governor Romer were all there. It was a great beginning.

"A committee of Rotarians was instrumental in hosting the banquet. For all their hard work, I made sure Denver Rotary got its own page on the program," Kinney added with a smile.

THE BRANCH RICKEY AWARD®

In February 1990, *Mile High Keyway* announced that the previous September's AOA opening night sales had topped $690,000, reversing a trend of diminishing sales that began in 1984. That year, Denver Rotary's *Artists of America* video won the Rocky Mountain Regional Emmy in the non-news category, adding to others from the New York and Houston Film Festivals and the U.S. Industrial Film Festivals in Chicago. Even so, many members expressed concern that interest in Artists of America might be waning.

"I was serving on the Board of Directors in 1991, when they asked me to chair an ad hoc committee to find a new fundraiser," said Jim Wilkins. "They felt that we needed another event, just in case AOA went away some day. Since we were already doing an arts event, the committee thought we should consider sports.

"I'd heard about Houston Rotary's Lombardi Award, which is still one of the top sports awards. I went down there twice and met with their committee," he said. "Their event, which is still going strong, raised money for a hospital for children with

cancer. I decided we should pattern our award after theirs, since they had been so successful. We thought about soccer first, but Roger Kinney, who was a member of our committee, suggested we take a look at Major League Baseball. Wilkins and his wife, Scotty, spent a good deal of time studying at the Denver Public Library before he recommended that the award be named in honor of Branch Rickey, a.k.a. "Mr. Baseball."

"Rickey was just an average player, but he excelled as a manager because he had a good mind and a passion for the game," said Wilkins. "He also had very high ethical standards. The owners hated him because he brought African Americans into baseball, starting with Jackie Robinson. Rickey made a number of contributions to the game, but more important, he was a great humanitarian who exemplifies what Rotary stands for—"Service Above Self."

Dave Winfield (Toronto Blue Jays) won the first Branch Rickey Award, presented by Bob Howsam on October 28, 1992. The event took place at a banquet cosponsored by Denver Rotary and the Colorado Rockies Club Baseball Foundation. Jim Wilkins looks on. Photo courtesy Denver Rotary Club.

On October 28, 1992, Dave Winfield of the Toronto Blue Jays won the first Branch Rickey Award, presented at a banquet cosponsored by Denver Rotary and the Colorado Rockies Club Baseball Foundation. More than five hundred Rotarians and fans turned out to celebrate Winfield, the forty-one-year-old "designated hitter" who scored a game-winning two-run double in the eleventh inning to win the 1992 World Series for Toronto. Inducted into the Baseball Hall of Fame in 2001, his first year of eligibility, Winfield would be the first active player to start his own charitable organization. More than $4 million of his own funds created the David M. Winfield Foundation, which deals with substance abuse problems in young people and operates a nutritional program for underprivileged children.

A Denver Post article on October 9, 1992, profiles Denver Rotary's first Branch Rickey Award recipient, Dave Winfield. Photo courtesy The Denver Post.

To select the annual Branch Rickey Award winner, each of the thirty major league teams submits the name of a nominee. A national voting panel of more than three hundred, including Major League Baseball executives, sportswriters, past recipients, and district governors in the cities where the teams reside, subsequently chooses a winner. The Branch Rickey Award, which inducts the selected player into the Baseball Humanitarian's Hall of Fame, has become one of baseball's most prestigious honors and a major fundraiser for Denver Rotary Club Foundation projects, principally Denver Kids, Inc. DKI has received almost $2.8 million in grants from the Foundation over the past twenty years, approximately half of the $5.4 million total grant funding.

BRANCH RICKEY, "MR. BASEBALL"

Born December 20, 1881, on an Ohio farm, Wesley Branch Rickey enrolled at Ohio Wesleyan University at nineteen, playing semiprofessional baseball and football to cover expenses. He spent a season with the Cincinnati Reds, but since he'd promised his mother that he would not play on Sundays, the team let him go. An average catcher for St. Louis Browns and the New York Yankees, his true genius lie in management. In 1912, as field manager for the St. Louis Browns, Rickey developed innovative methods that led him to be nicknamed a "professor of baseball." In 1917, he joined the St. Louis Cardinals, where he developed the "farm system," a brilliant plan that gave a major league clubs control of minor league franchises so that young players could perfect their skills before entering the majors. While working with the Cardinals, he has been credited with creating "the Knothole gang," which offered children free tickets to encourage their interest in baseball.

Jackie Robinson (left) and Branch Rickey were the team that changed baseball forever. Photo courtesy Denver Rotary Club.

In 1942, Rickey became the general manager of the Brooklyn Dodgers. A firm believer in desegregation, he chose Jackie Robinson, a former baseball, basketball, and All-American football star at UCLA, to become the first African American in the major leagues. Despite protests and discrimination from his own teammates, Robinson persevered. After Rickey made him the team's first baseman, Robinson led the Dodgers to the National League pennant. Both Robinson and Rickey have since become baseball legends.

Rickey became a prominent supporter of Civil Rights during the late 1940s, scheduling Dodger exhibitions in the South in defiance of segregation. After leaving the Dodgers in 1950, he worked briefly for the Pittsburgh Pirates and the St. Louis Cardinals baseball teams. On November 13, 1965, he collapsed from a heart attack during an acceptance speech while being inducted into the Missouri Sports Hall of Fame. He never regained consciousness and died on December 9, 1965.

Branch Rickey's grandson, Branch B. Rickey, is an honorary member of the Denver Rotary Club.

Rotarians honor the recipient at the Branch Rickey Award Dinner, now approaching its twentieth year. "We usually sell about five hundred to seven hundred tickets to the banquet," said Wilkins. "We select the winners because of their contributions to the community, like Bobby Valentine, who was one of the heroes of 9-11. We try to tie the event as closely to Rotary as we can."

On June 2, 2005, the Rotary Club of Denver unveiled *The Player,* a nine-foot, six-inch tall statue designed by sculptor George Lundeen. The bronze statue, dedicated to Branch Rickey and gifted to the Metropolitan Stadium District, displays the names of all award winners since 1992. Now a symbol of Coors Field, the statue sits atop a four-foot granite base at the stadium's main entrance, a public reminder of Denver Rotary's commitment to baseball and to the city of Denver.

BRANCH RICKEY AWARD WINNERS, 1982–2010

Craig Biggio (Houston Astros), 1997 winner of the Branch Rickey Award, shows kids from Denver Kids, Inc., how it's done. Photo courtesy Denver Rotary Club.

1992 Dave Winfield, Toronto Blue Jays
1993 Kirby Puckett, Minnesota Twins
1994 Ozzie Smith, St. Louis Cardinals
1995 Tony Gwynn, San Diego Padres
1996 Brett Butler, Los Angeles Dodgers
1997 Craig Biggio, Houston Astros
1998 Paul Molitor, Minnesota Twins
1999 Al Leiter, New York Mets
2000 Todd Stottlemyre, Arizona Diamondbacks
2001 Curt Schilling, Arizona Diamondbacks
2002 Bobby Valentine, New York Mets
2003 Roland Hemond, Chicago White Sox
2004 Jamie Moyer, Seattle Mariners
2005 Luis Gonzalez, Arizona Diamondbacks
2006 Tommy Lasorda, Los Angeles Dodgers
2007 John Smoltz, Atlanta Braves
2008 Trevor Hoffman, San Diego Padres
2009 Torii Hunter, Los Angeles Angels of Anaheim
2010 Vernon Wells, Toronto Blue Jays

Torii Hunter (California Angels) receives the 2009 Branch Rickey Award from Branch Rickey's grandson, Honorary Rotarian Branch B. Rickey, president of the Pacific Coast League. Photo courtesy Denver Rotary Club.

Left to right: Ozzie Smith, 1994 Branch Rickey Award winner, poses with Jim Wilkins and six-year-old Brian Mast, son of past president Steve Mast and Executive Director Darlene Mast. Now twenty-three, Brian has attended every Branch Rickey Award celebration since Kirby Puckett won in 1993. He has a baseball signed by all the winners. Photo courtesy Denver Rotary Club.

WORKING WITH YOUNG PEOPLE

Denver Boys, Denver Girls Merge to Become Denver Kids, Inc.

On September 24, 1993, *Mile High Keyway* announced that Denver Boys, Inc., and Denver Girls, Inc., had merged operations effective September 1. The new Denver Kids, Inc., would house operations at 740 Galapago Street. "It was the logical thing to do," said Donna Hultin, who began working with Denver Girls, Inc., in 1990 and retired as executive director of Denver Kids, Inc., in 2009. "The merger didn't change operations very much. Mentoring and long-term counseling programs remained gender specific, although we held many activities together."

The joint organization stayed true to its basic mission, serving Denver Public School children ages five through eighteen. Community volunteers served as role models and developed one-to-one relationships with the youngsters. Each full-time Denver Kids, Inc., educational counselor met with students weekly or bi-weekly to provide the stability often lacking in the child's life. Support services such as medical and dental assistance, financial aid and scholarships for camps or educational activities continued as before, and Denver Rotary, Denver Rotary Club Foundation, Denver Public Schools, and Zonta Club of Denver still provided support.

In 1988–89, the Youth Development Fund, which had been supported by voluntary contributions from Denver Rotarians, merged with the Denver Rotary Club Foundation, which took on responsibility for all youth programs. A key component in Denver Rotary's service to community children, Denver Kids, Inc., has received more than $3.8 million from the club since its inception.

Scholarships for Study Abroad

"Rotary offers several different types of scholarships for students who want to study outside the country," said Karl Berg, who served as district chair for ambassadorial scholarships during the early 1990s and still works on the scholarship committees. "For example, the Youth Exchange Committee, funded by the Denver Rotary Club Foundation, provides year-round international exchanges for high school students. Denver Kids often participate." The long-term program allows students ages sixteen to eighteen to study outside the country for approximately ten months. The ten-to-twelve-week summer program, which is more of an exchange, offers two sessions for students to spend five to six weeks in another country and a corresponding five to six weeks for families to host a student in their homes.

This 1994 publication applauds the Denver Kids, Inc. graduating class. Photo courtesy Denver Rotary Club.

Ambassadorial Scholar Akiko Shimohira poses with her parents, Ruyjiro (far right) and Kimie (far left), and Nancy Berg after graduation. Photo courtesy Karl Berg.

"Ambassadorial Scholarships, on the other hand, were founded by Rotary International in 1946 to promote international goodwill and understanding," he noted. "Every year, approximately seven to eight thousand students study abroad for a year as ambassadorial representatives of their country."

The selection process is fairly simple. Around June 1, the local clubs nominate one or two people in their districts for the award. In August, each district interviews the group (about twelve to fourteen) and selects two ambassadorial scholars. During their studies, the scholars connect with Rotary families near the campus but, unlike the high school students, they live in separate quarters. The amount of the award is $26,000/year for tuition, fees, room, and board, etc., which Berg said works out well in most countries.

"I remember one young woman, in particular, who taught me that, while interviewing these students, it's important not to make snap judgments based on outside appearance," he said. "I read her application, which seemed fine, but when the girl walked in, I thought she'd never make the grade. She looked too frivolous, a bit unkempt, like a hippie. It turned out she wanted to go to South Africa to work with the elephants, to help save them like Dian Fossey did with gorillas. She got the scholarship and did an excellent job.

"My wife and I became friends with another young lady from Japan, Akiko Shimohira, who was studying international relations at D.U.," he continued. "She now works for the Japanese government in Mozambique, and we still communicate. When her folks came here for her graduation, we all formed a lasting friendship, even though we spoke no Japanese and her parents spoke very little English."

Denver Rotary Youth Exchange student Armando Corona (front row, far left) visits with host families and committee members, including (back row, left to right) Charlie Miller, Mrs. Dawson, Ingrid Luszko, Steve Mast, Mr. Dawson, Darlene Mast, Lee White, Sue Fox, and Jim White. Seated next to Armando is friend Brian Mast and future outbound student Graham Dawson. Photo courtesy Denver Rotary Club.

Another ambassadorial scholarship is limited to architecture students, including urban planning, landscape design, etc. The Temple Buell Ambassadorial Scholarship also provides $26,000 for one academic year abroad. "The people we choose for this award are usually older, often in graduate school," said Berg. "We select students who are very focused, who we're pretty sure will make the grade."

Berg has been working with Ambassadorial Scholarships for nearly twenty years. "I often think I've been involved with this for too long, but honestly, these meetings with students are the best days of my year. It's a privilege working with really great young people."

WORLD COMMUNITY SERVICE COMMITTEE

Early Projects

In 1988, a small group of Denver Rotarians formed the first World Community Services Committee with $100 allocated to them from the Denver Rotary Club Foundation. By 1998, they had a budget of $23,000, a fifty-member committee and projects totaling over $2 million. Matching club funds with district and national funding, the committee managed to leverage financial support for projects around the world.

Rotarian Pete Wall recalls that it took awhile for the committee to find the right projects. "Since we had no formal structure, in the beginning we weren't quite sure what we were supposed to do," he admitted. "A group of professors from China were visiting CU-Denver, and someone suggested we invite them for lunch. That was our first project, such as it was."

The following year, John Lucken served as the committee chair. His wife, Mary, who worked for Denver Christian Schools, suggested that children in other countries might be able to use the school's old library books and a projector.

"The books would be dropped off at a warehouse," said Mike O'Connell, one of the project sponsors. "We held 'sorting Saturdays,' where club members helped us organize books according to topic, condition, etc. Then we boxed everything up to send to the Paraclete Government School at Grenada in the West Indies."

Unfortunately, the club had no funds for mailing. The committee approached the Denver Rotary Club Foundation, but they were uncertain about undertaking that type of project. "Finally Swede Johnson, an executive at Coors, got tired of all the discussion and just wrote a check," said Wall. "From 1993 to 1995 we shipped other supplies, including more books, a copier, computers, and a VCR."

After Lucken returned from a trip to the RI Convention in Mexico City, the club became involved with the small town of Ceylaya, Mexico, near Mexico City. In 1990, on behalf of the committee, the Denver Rotary Club Foundation presented John Hatch, president of the Foundation for International Community Assistance, with $2,500 to open the first FINCA (Foundation for International Community Assistance) Village bank, San Jose Las Flores. "It was the first time we formally applied to Denver Rotary Club Foundation for a grant," said O'Connell. The original loans included $50 each to thirty-five mothers, many of whom went into their own businesses. Some funds went toward home improvements, an important step in a town that had no sidewalks, streets, or sewage system.

Club President Joan Bristol and Rotarian Hank Strauss cofounded the Rotary Club of Vladivostok. Strauss credits Bristol with facing down the Russian mafia when they tried to confiscate a shipment of medical supplies she brought into the country. Strauss has led several projects, including the Lang Fang China Children's Center, which corrects cleft palates and heart defects. He assisted significantly with financing when RI ran out of funds for the project. Photo courtesy Denver Rotary Club.

"The women were good at keeping track of the money, so we put them in charge," Wall added. "They handled it very well—the payback rate is 99.98 percent." The club would sponsor two other banks in the 1990s, at Guadelupano, Mexico (1992), and Managua, Nicaragua (1997). In 1991, Rotary International awarded Denver Rotary District 5450 the RI Presidential Award of Honor in the category of World Community Service for support of Mexico.

Another effort in 1992 was not quite so successful. O'Connell, Lucken, and Wall learned that in Celaya, the poorest schools had no desks, and that the senior home needed more medical equipment. Rather than buying the desks, the committee decided to assemble tools and lumber, and a few members would drive down to Mexico to make sure the materials reached the right people. The committee applied to Rotary International for a Discovery Grant to cover basic travel expenses.

On October 29, 1993, the club purchased a Mercedes box truck, which Rotarians Wall, O'Connell, John and Mary Lucken, and Wills Long filled with tools and equipment, mostly donated by club members. With a large ROTARY decal painted on the side, they left for Mexico, having been assured by locals that the border crossing would be no problem. After spending a night at a Holiday Inn in El Paso, they headed for Mexico, accompanied by friends from Celaya Rotary.

THE GREAT BULLFIGHT

A visit to Celaya, Mexico, in the early 1990s, left Pete Wall with indelible memories. Photo courtesy John Lucken, photoshop courtesy Jamie Demmitt.

"After we finished the bank project, Mike O'Connell, John Lucken, and I went to down to Celaya to see what else we could do to help," said Pete Wall. "The Rotarians (Celaya Rotary District 416) were wonderful; they treated us like celebrities. They even held a picnic and a fiesta at a ranch owned by a retired matador. He had a bull ring, so the local matadors held demonstrations for us."

"They asked if any of us would like to give it a try," recalled O'Connell. "John and I politely declined, but Pete Wall volunteered. They gave him a short lesson, a hat, a cape, and a parade to lead him into the ring. He was supposed to 'fight' a baby bull, and by that I mean only three to four hundred pounds. It had tiny horns, though."

The crowd applauded as Wall stepped into the ring and prepared to do battle, more or less. "It ran right over me," he laughed. "I felt like I'd been tackled by a football player."

The bovine fullback subsequently jumped out of the ring, climbed into the stands, and crashed out into the parking lot, with the three Rotarians frantically chasing him through the crowd. Finally they herded the little fellow back to the pen. Fortunately, there were no casualties and only one bruised ego.

"I guess you could say Pete won," O'Connell laughed. "As far as I know, that was his last bullfight."

"When I drove the truck into Juarez, they wouldn't let us go any farther," Wall recalled, only half-humorously. "They had no idea that we were coming or what we were doing. We had to drive all the way back to the U.S. border. Naturally they didn't want to let us back into the United States with this huge truck, even in the days before 9-11. Finally the guards talked to some supervisor's supervisor, who told them to let us across. I found a Rotarian in Texas with an import/export business and left the truck with him. Although we talked a few times, nothing was ever resolved. I don't know to this day how it all worked out or if the truck ever made it back to Mexico."

NEPAL AND BEYOND

From 1992 to 1997, Denver Rotarians Dr. Francisco Sabichi, (Ph.D. Health Management) and Dr. Magdelyn (Lyn) Sabichi (physician, internal medicine) initiated the most ambitious project to date at the Koshi Zonal Hospital in Biratnegar, the second largest city in Nepal. Their initial assignment in 1992, a six-month medical project, led to a systematic overhaul of the hospital and a major local campaign for health education in one of the world's poorest countries.

"Having been to Nepal as a tourist, I was appalled by the conditions," said Lyn. "The people lived in horrible slums, in bamboo huts, where there's a complete lack of sanitation. At the time, 90 percent of the country had no running water."

The Sabichis worked as a team on administrative systems, since this was one of the hospital's greatest deficiencies. "In the beginning, we didn't know what to expect so we just kept quiet and observed," said Francisco, winner of the 1996–97 RI Service Above Self Award. "Before long, the administrator asked us for a report recommending ways in which the hospital could be improved. We made four suggestions: 1) purchase an X-ray machine, which was vital since Koshi is a referral hospital for the entire area; 2) begin a program of health education; 3) work on hospital infrastructure and water supply; and 4) build housing for the orderlies and hospital personnel.

"Southeast Nepal lies at sea level on India's southern plains, which flood every year," he explained. "There's a lot of illness, particularly malaria, so it's preferable for hospital staff to live on site." Also, the hospital badly needed structural improvements. "Even the sinks and toilets were dysfunctional, which is unbelievable for a hospital," Lyn observed.

To begin their work, they needed $25,000, which Denver Rotary Club Foundation and clubs in the district provided. With a Rotary 3-H Grant (Health, Hunger, and Humanity) and assistance from individual donors, the RI Foundation and the Denver Club Rotary Foundation, they eventually raised $350,000. "The local Rotarians gave us a lot of support," said Francisco. "Getting the simplest things done can be a huge problem in these countries, and they knew how to deal with local labor and acquire materials, among other things."

A Health Education Program was vital, starting with physicians and administrators. When the Sabichis arrived nearly eighteen years ago, they estimated the literacy rate in Nepal, particularly for women in rural areas, at approximately 10 percent. (In 2007, the Human Development Index estimated 56 percent, with

During the annual changing of the guard, incoming DRC President Joan Bristol, 2000–2001, presents outgoing President Jim Mack, 1999–2000, with "Billy Bass," a mechanical talking fish whose significance has been lost over the years. Photo courtesy Denver Rotary Club.

higher rates for men in the cities.) Without written communication, they were forced to develop innovative educational methods, including street plays acted out by the health team, announcements on loudspeakers, colorful posters with drawings and messages on movie screens ("Movies are very popular," said Francisco. "There's not much else to do for entertainment.") They also created a mobile library, so that health information could be available for patients in waiting rooms. Staff gave immunization cards to women who brought their children into the hospital. After awhile, the mothers began to request them. The biggest challenge, however, would be teaching the people to wash their hands.

"We needed to follow up into the community to understand what might prevent people from washing their hands, like working in the fields all day with no access to clean water," Lyn said. "Along with the street plays, the women at the hospital would perform hand-washing demonstrations, which would draw big crowds. We tried to make it fun."

By May 2003, progress was evident. In an article in *The Rotarian*, Lyn maintained that the entire community had become more health conscious. "We're trying to make them aware of things they can do to improve sanitation," she said. "We're seeing a tremendous improvement."

The Sabichis have since spearheaded similar projects in Ethiopia, India, Russia, and the Far East. "For Rotary volunteers in these countries, the issues are much the same," Francisco continued. "Lack of adequate health care services and ignorance of cleanliness are always problematic. The people are fabulous to work with, though, and that's what makes it all worthwhile."

Lyn and Francisco Sabichi are shown here accepting the Rotary International Foundation Award. Tom Craine stands at left. Photo courtesy Denver Rotary Club.

GROWTH OF DENVER ROTARY CLUB FOUNDATION

During Denver Rotary's Fiscal Year 1993–94, the club created a Foundation's Membership Committee to pursue programs and projects that would help members understand the differences between the Denver Rotary Club Foundation and the Rotary International Foundation. The club subsequently installed new databases and accounting systems to gather updated information from members of each foundation; membership subsequently increased in both foundations. By July 1, 1997, the Denver Rotary Club Foundation included 242 fellows and 260 sustaining members from a total club membership of 625. In 1996–97, the Foundation adopted a new logo, "Hands Reaching to the Stars," which is now used on recognition pins at various levels of giving.

Childhood Literacy Committee member Bud Figel reads to student at Munroe Elementary in 1996. Photo courtesy Denver Rotary Club.

CLUB NOTES

Denver Rotary would make its own changes during the 1990s. On May 29, 1994, the club moved to new offices in the Bank Western Building at 718 Seventeenth Street, although meetings still were held at the Denver Athletic Club.

Mile High Keyway remained the club's primary method of communication. In July 1992, a cheery gossip column called "Heard Around the Club" made a very brief appearance and quickly faded away, but not before offering snippets such as: "So what did Club Secretary Dennis Graham hook when he rigged up his recently acquired fly rod and stalked the wily trout? Only his waders know for sure."

To cover rising printing costs, Denver Rotary began a series of advertising promotions in 1993–94, charging for $35 to $45 per ad per issue. Members also were encouraged to submit a 250-word company profile to the new "Spotlight on Business" column. Before long, however, technology would lead the way toward a less expensive paperless publication.

Rotarian Larry Bohning, a Denver County Court Judge, served as club secretary under Mike O'Connell, Bob Kapelke and Becky Mallory. During his "warm-up acts" for the presidents, Bohning often spoofed "Carnac the Magnificent" inspired by longtime television comedian Johnny Carson. During his travels in the East, "Carnac" supposedly learned "how to cloud men's minds." He would characteristically give an answer and then open a sealed envelope and read the question. Example: Answer: 20,000 Leagues Beneath the Sea. Question: Where is the American dollar headed? Photo courtesy Denver Rotary.

On May 6, 1998, Denver Rotary proudly unveiled the club's first website, www. rotary-denver.31.org, later changed to www.denverrotary.org. The new Website featured a calendar of events, *Mile High Keyway* newsletters past and present, links to RI and District 5450 and membership information. Even in the tech-savvy late 1990s, however, readers were warned to visit the "Need Help" link first.

"We strongly recommend that you first read online and print or download," *Keyway* advised.

WHAT IS A ROTARIAN?

A Rotarian is a person who digs wells from which he won't drink
A person who vaccinates children he will never meet
Who restores eyesight to those he won't ever see
Who builds housing he will never live in
Who educates people he will never know
Who plants trees he will never see or sit under
Who feeds hungry people, regardless of
color, race or politics
Who makes crawlers into walkers halfway
around the world
Who knows real happiness,
which as Albert Schweitzer
said, "can only be found
by serving others."
　　　—Grant Wilkins, Denver
　　　　Rotary Club 31

Rotarian Elrey P. Jeppesen (left) poses with sculptor George Lundeen next to the sixteen-foot bronze statue of the aviator in leather pilot's helmet, goggles, and jodhpurs sculpted in 1993. The statue now stands near the north security screening lines at Denver International Airport, which opened in 1995. For nervous passengers, "Jepp" has a positive connection to air travel. Photo courtesy George Lundeen.

Capt. E.B. Jeppese
AND SCULPTUR on
GEORGE LUNDEEN
at LUNDEEN STUD
LOVELAND COLORA

CHAPTER VIII

Changing Times
2000–2010

DENVER IN THE 2000s

As the new millennium approached, Denver Metro area residents looked toward the future with optimism. The economic boom of the 1990s ushered in a promising era of growth in the business community, particularly around the bustling Denver Tech Center area and the new Interlocken Business Park along the I-36 corridor. Downtown, developers and their architects proposed new projects in the Central Platte Valley behind Union Station, including a thirty-acre Commons Park with wetlands and trails along the South Platte River.

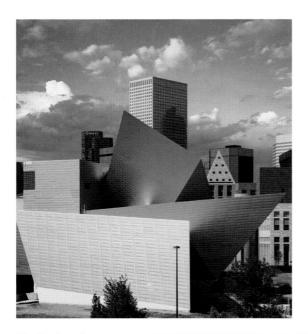

During the previous decade, many older downtown buildings were restored and refurbished with help from the Colorado State Historical Fund, subsidized by gaming tax revenue from Black Hawk, Cripple Creek, and Central City. Improvements along Seventeenth Street, which had borne the brunt of the oil industry demise, were funded with help from the Downtown Denver Partnership.

The organization's founder, longtime Rotarian Philip Milstein, had been among the many club members who belonged to the Partnership, originally called Downtown Denver, Inc. Milstein has been credited with the idea for the pedestrian Sixteenth Street Mall, which was completed in the 1980s.

From 1991 to 2003, Rotarian Wellington Webb served the city as Denver's first African American mayor. Webb dealt with several headaches inherited from the previous administration, including the airport baggage system, but preferred to focus on parks and open space, economic development, and programs for children.

The Frederic C. Hamilton addition to the Denver Art Museum (North Building) made its debut in 2006. Photo courtesy VISIT DENVER: The Convention and Visitors Bureau.

The Centennial Statue at the entrance to Coors Field, The Player, *was dedicated June 2, 2005. Looking on are Branch B. Rickey (left), Mayor John Hickenlooper, and Grant Wilkins. Photo courtesy Denver Rotary Club.*

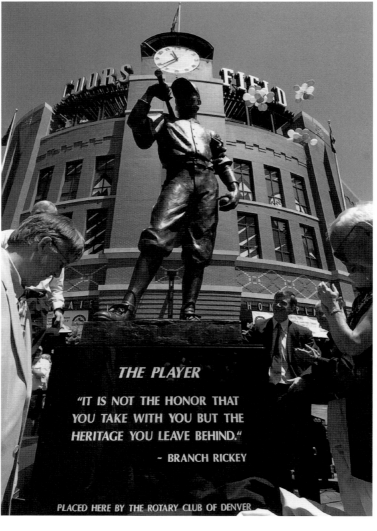

His administration saw the completion of substantial investments in Denver's infrastructure, such as the Colorado Convention Center, the Denver Central Library, Coors Field, and the Pepsi Center.

The revitalization of LoDo (the Lower Downtown District), the opening of the relocated Elitch Gardens (1994–95), and the Denver Pavilions retail and entertainment center (1998) all brought tourists and suburbanites downtown in numbers unthinkable twenty years earlier. The arts flourished during the 2000s as the old Denver Municipal Auditorium became the Ellie Caulkins Opera House and the

Frederick C. Hamilton addition to the Denver Art Museum opened in October 2006. Denver's last substantial chunks of real estate ripe for new development, the former Lowry Air Force Base and Stapleton Airport (both closed in the mid-1990s) were becoming mixed residential/commercial areas, the latter to the tune of more than $4 billion.

The only blip on the horizon, the rumor of an impending "Y2K" disaster, captured the public's attention months before the clock struck midnight December 31, 1999. Since older time-sensitive computers had been programmed to store only two-digit numbers for each calendar year, fears abounded that the year 2000 would be read as 1900, leading data systems and computers to fail or malfunction. Even the most skeptical stocked up on water and basics in the event that civilization came to a screeching halt. As it turned out, either the computer industry got a handle on the problem early or the situation had been exaggerated, but the world greeted the year 2000 with systems functioning.

The first sign of future economic woes appeared March 10, 2000, when a NASDAQ crash followed the collapse of the dot-com bubble. Since multiple dot.com or Internet-based companies had nested in the Denver–Colorado Springs area, the Front Range would be hard hit as the bonanza of the previous decade morphed into a recession. Many companies either folded or relocated, particularly in Denver Tech Center, which had been occupied nearly to capacity. The office vacancy rate

The Pepsi Center hosted multiple events for the Democratic National Convention of 2008. Photo courtesy VISIT DENVER: The Convention and Visitors Bureau.

in Denver would reach a staggering 25 percent, a level unseen since oil bust of the 1980s. Foreclosures increased as nearly sixty thousand people lost their jobs.

On September 11, 2001, the attacks on the World Trade Center and the Pentagon led to the bankruptcy of United Airlines, a major local employer. Tourism, Colorado's second largest industry, would also suffer from a series of wildfires that accompanied a major drought from 2000 to 2003. The Hayman disaster of 2002, the largest fire in the state's history, burned 138,000 acres south and west of Denver, polluting the atmosphere with reddish-orange smog that hovered over the city for days. Even so, 26 million people took overnight trips to Colorado that year, nearly 3 million swarming like butterflies over Rocky Mountain National Park.

Politically, Denverites remained firmly in the Democratic camp. Promising an efficient city government, Rotarian John Hickenlooper won the mayoral elections in 2003 and 2007. A relative political unknown, Hickenlooper had been involved with numerous downtown Denver renovation and development projects, particularly

The new University of Colorado Anschutz Medical Campus currently includes the University of Colorado Health Sciences Center, University of Colorado Hospital, and Children's Hospital, which has begun a $228 million expansion. The U.S. Department of Veteran's Affairs Hospital broke ground on the campus in 2009. Photo courtesy Tom Noel.

in lower downtown. By April 2005, *Time* magazine had named him one of the top five "big-city" mayors in America. Although both Hickenlooper and Denver won kudos for money-saving innovations in government, landing the 2008 Democratic National Convention would be the coup. The largest convention in Denver's history, the DNC attracted approximately fifty thousand people, resulting in an economic windfall for the city of approximately $160 million. Propelled by such successes, Hickenlooper became Colorado's forty-second governor in 2011.

Despite the economic crunch, new buildings would grace the Denver skyline for the first time in nearly two decades, beginning in 2005 with the thirty-seven-story Hyatt Regency Denver at the Colorado Convention Center Hotel. Others included a twenty-two-story office building at 1800 Larimer, which proclaimed itself the most energy-efficient building downtown, the thirty-two-story One Lincoln Park, the forty-one-story Spire residential condominium buildings, and the forty-five-story Four Seasons Hotel and Residences. The growing desirability of downtown living, first demonstrated by the popularity of restored LoDo lofts and condominiums in the 1990s, led to the addition of nearly eleven thousand new units in the 2000s.

Other major construction during the decade took place farther east, as Fitzsimmons Army Medical Center that was decommissioned in 1995 became part of the new University of Colorado Anschutz Medical Campus. The hospital and research megaplex currently includes the University of Colorado Health Sciences Center, University of Colorado Hospital, and Children's Hospital, which plans a $228-million expansion just a few years after opening. The U.S. Department of Veteran's Affairs Hospital broke ground on the campus in 2009.

That same year, just two months short of its 150th birthday, the *Rocky Mountain News* published its final edition on February 27. The closure, which some had anticipated since the joint operating agreement between the *News* and *The Denver Post* in 2000, left the city with only one daily paper with a large circulation. Many mourned the loss of Denver's oldest newspaper, which had chronicled Denver's ups and downs beginning on April 23, 1859, at the height of the Pikes Peak Gold Rush. Even after winning four Pulitzer Prizes since 2000, the *News,* like many papers around the country, fell victim to the recession and accompanying loss of ad revenue. Newspaper readership dropped during the decade as, according to a CNN survey, more Americans began to get their news via the Internet. Individuals under thirty-five, in particular, preferred e-mail or updates on social media sites like Facebook or Twitter as the technological stranglehold on the younger generation tightened.

Despite a brief economic recovery in late 2003, the city and state faced a much more serious global recession, beginning in 2007 and reverberating into the next decade. In the early days of the economic disaster, Colorado briefly became the foreclosure capital of the country. Despite hard times, according to 2010 U.S Census, the state's population grew by almost 17 percent from 2000 to 2010, the ninth largest increase in the country. Denver kept pace, increasing from 554,636 in 2000 to approximately 625,000 residents ten years later. As inner-city decay of earlier decades gave way to an urban renaissance, the 2000s marked the second decade of Denver's steady growth since the 1970s retreat to the suburbs.

MODIFICATIONS AND MILESTONES

The club experienced its own changes as globalization struck home and more businesses moved out of state or sometimes out of the country. As other Rotary clubs proliferated in the Denver Metro area, Club 31 membership decreased from 541 in June 2000 to 330 in 2010. The club's constituency, once the domain of CEOs and corporate giants, now included many self-employed individuals, middle-level managers, and representatives from charitable foundations.

Paul Harris looks on in spirit as Al Brenman (left), 2006–2007 RI President William Boyd, past District Governor Tallee Crowe, and Dean Laudeman chat during the annual visit of the RI president to Denver Rotary, where Paul Harris recipients/donors were honored. Photo courtesy Denver Rotary Club.

"In some ways, I think Denver Rotary accomplishes more now than we did with a membership of six hundred," said Grant Wilkins. "When I was president in 1978–79, we had only a few Paul Harris Fellows; now there are hundreds. We had no world community service. We were involved in two or three projects, whereas today we take on thirty or more."

In 2008, Denver Rotary was named the best service club on National Philanthropy Day. Second row, left to right: Todd Bacon, Steve Mast, Marie Wheatley, Bill Houston, Roland Thornton, and Chuck Everill. Front row, left to right: Darlene Mast, Donna Hultin, Sue Fox, and R. J. Ross. Photo courtesy Denver Rotary Club.

"Between 2000 and 2007, there were few changes in day-to-day operations, other than the addition of one or two club positions," said Steve Mast, Denver Rotary president in 2003–04. "However, some members began to complain about time required for monthly meetings, which lasted from noon to 1:30 p.m. The longer meetings gave us the opportunity to sit and talk and get to know each other better. We experimented with a variety of styles, but finally reduced the meetings to one hour, which doesn't leave much time for socialization. We try to meet that need through social activities and the Fellowship Meetings, where smaller groups are involved."

With the goal of finding a permanent home for the office, which moved often since the Cosmopolitan Hotel demolition in 1984, Denver Rotary purchased a street-level condominium downtown.

"We placed a contract on the 1350 Lawrence Street condo in August 2000 and moved in on December 21," said Darlene Mast, executive director since July 2004. "As it turned out, we didn't need quite so much space. Since the market was right, we sold the condominium on January 16, 2007, and moved to our current location at 1900 Grant Street, Suite 850, on April 1."

Roland Thornton (far right) made the news when he became the first African American president of Denver Rotary in 2008–2009. This photo was taken during a 2009 visit to RI headquarters with Grant Wilkins (not pictured). RI President John Kenny stands center and District Governor Mike Oldham is on the left. Photo courtesy Denver Rotary Club.

On August 3–4, 2007, Denver welcomed the Rotary International President's Conference on Membership at the Denver Sheraton Four Points. Speakers included Ron Beaubien, chair of the RI Membership Committee, who stressed Rotary's need to connect and become relevant to younger people, a.k.a. Gen X (born 1965–1984) and Gen Y (1985–2010). Interpreting his remarks, Denver Rotary wordsmith Irina Buckley Hopkins wrote in *Mile High Keyway*, "Gen X demands a role in formation, not just execution. They want variety and are unlikely to stick to the same old, same old." Hopkins added that the younger generations want to give time and talent, not just a check, and that they crave challenge and social connectivity. "We need to redefine the brand, and in this case, the brand is Rotary."

In 2008, National Philanthropy Day, which is supported by the Association of Fundraising Professionals and hundreds of nonprofit and for-profit organizations throughout North America, named Rotary Club of Denver the year's Outstanding Service Organization. The award is presented to a service organization that has demonstrated outstanding commitment through financial support and the encouragement and motivation of others to take leadership roles in philanthropy and community involvement.

The club reached another milestone in 2009–2010 after electing its first African American president, Roland R. Thornton, executive vice president of Wholesale Marketing for Qwest Communications. Thornton told *The Denver Post* and Channel 9 News, "Our world is becoming more global and more diverse, and Rotary must keep up with that trend if we're to remain relevant in our society today. We've stayed the course too long on the old model. The new generation of available members is more tech-savvy, involved in social networking, and Rotary has to move to them."

New technology also affected the way the club communicated with its members. In 1998, *Mile High Keyway* and other club information became available online. To save money and "stay green," the club subsequently stopped mailing paper copies in 2009. The newsletter format has remained much the same, with news briefs, information on guest speakers and "Birthatarians" duly noted. "The Observer" column, although no longer anonymous, still appears regularly.

In 2007, Denver Rotary's new Website debuted as www.rotary-denver31.org.

THE SOCIAL SCENE

Along with various mixers and gathering, the club holds annual social events for members and their families. Two family-oriented celebrations date back to the club's infancy—the Annual Picnic and the Holiday Party. Usually held at Elitch Gardens, the picnic rotated around various locales during the early years, including Evans Park and even Olinger Mortuary grounds. More recent venues have included the Denver Zoo and Four Mile Historic Park.

Santa, a.k.a. Eric White, and his Rotarian helpers take a time out at the 2008 Holiday Party. Pictured left to right: Thanh Nguyen, Ahden Busch, Carol Duncan, and Nancy Austin. Photo courtesy Denver Rotary Club.

Holiday Parties, once celebrated at the old Albany, Cosmopolitan, and Denver Hilton Hotels would be held primarily at the Denver Athletic Club. Besides providing entertainment and gifts for the kids, in past years the celebration has allowed youngsters the opportunity to help run the meeting, giving the future generation a taste of Rotary workings.

Club members continue to enjoy the annual Family Rotary Day at the Rockies and Rotary Night at the National Western Stock Show and Rodeo. A Tango-Fandango Dance in 2009 restored the traditional dinner/dance social event.

Although the musical Stag Night programs of the 1920s have gone the way of the Valentine's Day Dance and Ladies Night, humor and a love of music have always characterized Denver Rotarians. In 2005, Bob Kapelke, former Colorado Court of Appeals judge, club president, and author of *Twelfth Night* skits for the University Club, followed the tradition when he created *Rotary, the Musical,* a good-natured spoof of all things Rotarian. Kapelke and crew took the show on the road to the Rotary International 100th Anniversary celebration in Evanston, where club member Charlie Miller played Paul Harris. To keep members on their toes, Kapelke's musical entourage has been entertaining audiences at Denver Rotary's annual April Fool's Day meeting. The performers satirize everyone from the Broncos to "Hillary Clinton," played in 2009 by U.S. Assistant Attorney Brenda Taylor, who warbles a political lament to the strains of *Blues in the Night [Obama done told me . . .].* The *April Fool's Walk of 2009* can be viewed online via YouTube.

Rotarian Harriet Downer, dressed in witches' garb, hands out treats at DCIS's annual "Truck or Treat" for the neighborhood kids. Photo courtesy Denver Rotary Club.

Rotarians (left to right) Doug McLemore and Will Snider strum away at the 2009 Family Picnic at 4-Mile House. Photo courtesy Denver Rotary Club.

Denver Rotarians enjoy the Rotary Picnic at the Rockies in 2008. Seated far left, front row, is the club's most senior member (for nearly sixty years) Rex Post. Photo courtesy Denver Rotary Club.

140

"We've always had fun," said Sue Fox, Denver Rotary president in 2008–09. "I remember when Ed Crabtree served as programs chair. He started a rumor that Ward Churchill [controversial CU-Boulder professor] might be invited to the luncheon as a guest speaker. We were deluged with emails, some for and some against, more than we ever received about anything else. Even after we announced that it was an April Fool's Day joke, people were still emailing their opinions."

On June 26, 2008, outgoing Club President Doug Jackson auctioned off the club presidency for six days, since he would be out of the country before Sue Fox took over on July 2. The winner of the "President for Almost a Week" Award, Bob Lowdermilk made a generous donation to the club's foundation, to be point-matched by the DRCF for an honor that that came with "no authority, no decision-making ability, and pay way below minimum wage."

"In the meantime," stated *Mile High Keyway*, "the club executive director is reviewing the by-laws to make sure this can be done. She expects this process to last about six days."

Club president Steve Mast waves to the crowd at the National Western Stock Show while Bob Kapelke rides shotgun. Photo courtesy Denver Rotary.

Bob Kapelke and crew keep Rotarians laughing with their annual April Fools Day musical. Front row, left to right: Bob Kapalka and Tom Rogers. Back row: Phil Heinschel, John Howell, John McLagen, Bob Fawcett, Dennis Graham, and Bill Chenoweth. Photo courtesy Denver Rotary Club.

Stars of the Rotary, the Musical *perform at the Changing of the Guard Program at Cherry Hills Country Club in July 2008.*

Denver Rotarians have been involved with the stock show since the early years. Photo courtesy VISIT DENVER: The Convention and Visitors Bureau.

Sue Fox became president of Denver Rotary Club in 2008, the same year that her husband, Bob Martin, was elected president of the Highlands Ranch Rotary Club. To date, they are the only married couple to serve simultaneous terms as club presidents in Rotary history. Let the party begin! Photo courtesy Sue Fox.

Club President Doug Jackson (right) shakes hands with Bob Lowdermilk, "Club President for Six Days" between the official "Changing of the Guard" in July 2008. Photo courtesy Denver Rotary Club.

THE DENVER ROTARY CLUB FOUNDATION EVOLVES

Partly as a result of the economic instability of the early 2000s, Denver Rotary Club Foundation President Jim Wilkins and Treasurer Rike Wootten updated the formula used for calculating grantable funds in 2003–04. "We were hitting these tremendous peaks and valleys depending on the year's proceeds, what the economy was doing, and what the portfolio looked like," Wilkins said. "We needed a new way of doing things."

The Denver Rotary Club Foundation subsequently modified the formula to level out despite market fluctuations, basing annual funding on (a) 50 percent of member contributions from prior fiscal year; (b) plus 50 percent of fundraisers, such as the Annual Peach Sale; (c) plus 100 percent of direct contributions (Branch Rickey); (d) plus 4.5 percent of the corpus. Under Wooten's tutelage, the DRCF hired the first asset management trust company, which for the majority of the decade has been AMG National Trust Bank.

"The grants review process became significantly more sophisticated," added Chuck Everill, 2009–2010 Denver Rotary Club Foundation president. "We can now go back to organizations we like and give them some guidance. For example, Scholastic Arts has a long history with the club. When we saw the core arts organization withering, we asked Todd Bacon [former AOA chair] to help them change their board structure. The revitalized organization now supports seventeen hundred Colorado students annually. It has phenomenal impact."

According to Pete Wall, the Grants Committee process began to evolve with DRCF President Garth Grissom in 1989–1990. "At one time, the club thought it could tell the Foundation what to do," Wall commented. "Garth, being a lawyer, insisted that they are two different organizations. Now we have representation on the Grants Committee from the Board, the club at large, and the Denver Rotary Foundation, while the trustees have final fiduciary obligation." The Foundation's trustees meet bi-monthly and the Executive Committee meets on alternate months, usually via conference call.

"In the approval process we also maintain the ability to respond to emergency requests," said 2010–2011 DRCF President Frank Lawrence. "It's a small piece of our distribution and the effort requires Rotarian involvement. He added that this ability stands independently from normal grant requests, controlled by a separate set of guidelines.

Summing up, Lawrence observed that the past ten years have shown a significant maturing of the Foundation. "Infrastructures such as procedures, investment policy, giving level recognitions and granting guidelines are much more formalized," he said. "What's important, however, is that grants from Denver Rotary Club Foundation change people's lives. That's what it's all about."

DENVER ROTARY CLUB FOUNDATION GRANTS, 2011–2012

College Counseling Initiative—$20,000
Provides college counseling and financial resources to Denver Kids, Inc., High School Scholarship recipients and DCIS students.

Community Resources, Inc. (Youth Mentoring)—$11,000
Matches gifted at-risk students in grades four through eight with accomplished community/Rotarian volunteers for a short-term academic/career project.

Randy Dunn (far left) accompanies students from Denver Rotary's Adopt-a-School, the Denver Center for International Studies, on a trip to visit the United Nations in 2007. Photo courtesy Denver Rotary Club.

Denver Center for International Studies/Interact (DCIS)—$10,000
Provides Centennial Adopt-a-School Project with resources, both financial and human, to the students, faculty/staff to improve student performance and provide access to international opportunities. DCIS is also home to the Club's Interact Club.

Denver Kids, Inc.—$140,000
Helps support one thousand at-risk Denver Public School students through DKI's mentoring and counseling program.

Branch Rickey Award recipient John Smoltz (2007) is seen here surrounded by the many faces of Denver Kids. Photo courtesy Denver Rotary Club.

Global Health Connections—$6,000

An educational outreach program that brings middle school students in Colorado and worldwide together to work on multicultural solutions to global heath issues.

The Harmony Project—$2,500

Provides an integrated arts program in underserved schools (DCIS) by pairing classroom teachers with a professional artist, together working as a team to create a plan for integrating the art form into the curriculum.

High School Scholarship and Achievement Awards—$20,000

Provides thirty economically disadvantaged high school juniors/ seniors with financial assistance ($60 a month) and Rotarian mentorship during the school year.

Junior Achievement—$3,500

An innovative program that enables fifteen to eighteen teams of Rotarian members and DCIS Interact Club students to team-teach Junior Achievement programs at a DPS elementary school.

Students of Hill Middle School competed in the 2008 Denver Water Challenge hosted by Global Health Connections, a grant recipient of the Denver Rotary Club Foundation. Photo courtesy Denver Rotary Club.

Rotary Youth Leadership Award (RYLA)—$5,200

Allows ten high school and five middle school students to participate in a summer Rotary leadership camp in Estes Park.

Scholastic Art Awards Colorado—$8,000

Continued Rotary sponsorship of the annual Colorado art exhibit in which more than seventeen hundred high school art students participate.

Shining Stars—$3,500

Provides activities for children and young adults with cancer at the Shining Stars Winter Games in Aspen.

Vocational College Scholarships—$15,000

Provides educational scholarships to students in vocational, trade, and technical fields, and a Rotarian/student mentoring program.

World Community Service Committee—$34,000

Provides funds for more than thirty Rotarian recommended/driven humanitarian projects in more than twenty countries around the world. Many projects are leveraged more than three to one.

Youth Exchange Committee—$3,000

Hosts incoming/outbound students throughout the world, providing year-long international exchanges at the high school level.

Total Grants for 2011–2012—$281,200

The Denver Rotary Club Foundation supports the Shining Stars Foundation Winter Games. Front row, left to right: Mikee and Bob Kapelke, Scotty Wilkins, Pete Wall, Mary Underwood, and Larry Gloss. Back row, left to right: Brian and Amy Blankenburg, Jim Wilkins, and Will Snider. Photo courtesy Shining Stars.

In June 2008, Denver Rotary's World Community Service Committee provided financial assistance for students from North High School to travel to an orphanage and school in San Miguel and assist in maintenance projects. Photo courtesy Denver Rotary Club.

SCHOLASTIC ARTS AND WRITING AWARDS COLORADO

The Scholastic Arts and Writing Awards date back to 1923, the oldest, longest-running and most prestigious scholarship and recognition program in visual arts and writing in the United States. At this time, Colorado participates only in the visual arts part of the program.

"Through the Colorado Art Education Association, art teachers from high schools around the state encourage their students to submit a portfolio to be judged by a committee," explained Frank Lawrence. "Winners are recognized at various levels, and there's an art show at the Rocky Mountain Arts Institute. [In 2011, the Denver Art Museum hosted the exhibit.] Top winners go on to a national competition in Washington, D.C."

"Years ago, the teachers made the decisions, but now everything is done online," added Chuck Everill. "It's the national championship for artists, a way for Colorado art students to gain recognition. The winners receive college scholarships from other organizations, not just Rotary—several hundred thousands of dollars from art institutes and schools. Had Rotary not stepped in to resurrect the group, these students would not have access to the scholarships."

Internationally recognized past winners include Quang Ho, one of the country's most recognized representational artists and the first place Gold Key scholarship winner in 1982.

Born in 1963, the artist immigrated to the United States from Vietnam with his family in 1975. His early aptitude for art led him to enroll in the Colorado Institute of Art in 1982, thanks to the Scholastic Arts Scholarship. That same year, the artist's mother was killed in an auto accident, leaving him with the responsibility of raising five younger siblings. The scholarship enabled him to complete his education and continue on his career path.

Renowned artist Quang Ho (left), Scholastic Arts scholarship winner, poses with former AOA chair Todd Bacon. Photo courtesy Todd Bacon.

In a moving speech at the 2010 Denver Rotary Club Foundation Celebration Day, the artist recalled a phone call from Preston Smith shortly after receiving the award, inviting him to the Artists of America Show. "I had always learned art from books, and had never seen a real painting hung in a gallery," he said. He later became one of AOA's best selling artists, whose works have been exhibited and held in collections in America and abroad.

At the event, Quang Ho credited Denver Rotary with his later successes. "If it had not been for Rotary, I would not have been able to go to that school," he said. "It changed the course of my life."

DENVER ROTARY SPONSORS THE FIRST CYBER CLUB

At a Quad District Foundation dinner in Denver on January 18, 2002, RI President-elect Bhichai Rattakul recognized the first internet-based Rotary Club in history, eClub One of District 5450. The original Website, www.rotary5450.

org/eclub, has since been changed to www.rotaryeclubone.org. According to the club's first president, John Minter, twelve hours (or thirteen quarters) of community or international service would be required in place of seat time in a terra club (attending regular meetings). Members would determine their own activities, time, and place.

The pilot program became particularly popular with individuals with disabilities and members in remote locations or those with demanding travel schedules. Regular members who wished to make up a meeting were required to spend thirty minutes on site, reading from a collection of programs, and complete a make-up request form. As one Rotarian who recently had open-heart surgery commented on the Website, "Being able to make up meetings helped me to keep perfect attendance for more than forty years."

Rotary eClub One averages between fifty and sixty members at any one time. E-clubs usually required a donation commensurate with payment at a regular meeting.

By April 26, 2010, when RI granted permanent status to the program, 360 Rotarians belonged to fourteen e-clubs around the world. In District 5450, projects range from Educate!, which helps scholars develop social enterprise systems in Uganda, to the Second Wind Foundation, a suicide-prevention program for teens in the United States. EClub One now includes sixty-one Paul Harris Fellowships, twenty-one Multiple Paul Harris Fellowships and six benefactors to the Permanent Fund.

A ROTARY GLOSSARY
Excerpt from Mile High Keyway, *August 28, 1992.*

1. rotarrhea: an affliction in which one can't stop talking about Rotary
2. rotaregular: a Rotarian with perfect attendance
3. rota-rooter: an avid booster of Rotary
4. rotasaurus: a very old Rotarian
5. rotanoia: fear that Rotary is taking over one's life
6. rotaholic: one whose life has already been taken over
7. rotadiction: an affliction in which one cannot speak without using rotarisms
8. rotarrific: wonderful in a special, Rotary way
9. rotacrastinate: to put off doing committee duties until the last possible minute
10. rotavision: the belief that service, fellowship, and weekly meetings can make the world a better place.

The community of Zozokodzi in Togo, West Africa, expresses thanks during a ribbon-cutting ceremony for a new well. Funded by a Denver Rotary World Community Service matching grant led by Pete Wall, this endeavor won the George Davis Water Project Award at the 2007 District Conference. Photo courtesy Denver Rotary Club.

WORLD COMMUNITY SERVICE COMMITTEE WORKINGS

The World Community Services Committee receives an annual budget for new projects from the Denver Rotary Foundation, $40,000 in 2010–2011. During monthly meetings, the committee listens to and votes upon proposals for new activities and reviews reports on the status of ongoing projects. Each project must have a "champion" within the committee, who provides suggestions and may solicit contributions from other clubs. He or she presents the proposal to the committee for approval and processes the paperwork.

PEACHES, PEACHES

Along with the Branch Rickey Award Dinner in September, the Annual Peach Sale has become a favorite club gathering, now going into its eighth year. According to real estate broker John (Jay) Yake, who chairs the committee with his wife, Carol Duncan (together known as Peach and Pit), the idea for a peach sale originated with the Rotary Club of Golden and filtered down when one of their members joined Club 31.

During the year, Rotarians take orders for fresh freestone peaches, which are delivered to the Denver Center for International Studies (DCIS) on the last Saturday in August. "The peaches are picked late Friday night and delivered to us Saturday morning, so they're really fresh. We're usually open for business from about 8 a.m. until 12:30 p.m.," Yake said.

Although most orders come from Rotarians, their friends and families, anyone can purchase a case, and last year the club began accepting orders online. George I. (Skip) Ahern, Jr., has held the title "Peach King" for the past three years, having sold as many as 110 cases.

In 2008, Channel 9 *Morning News* covered the event, allowing club president Sue Fox and the DCIS Interact president to raise public awareness of Rotary activities. "We had cars lined up around the block, and we quickly ran out of peaches, but it was great publicity," Yake said. The club has since offered walk-up customers fresh peaches for $10 a bag.

Denver Rotarians unloaded 1,670 boxes of peaches at the 2008 Peach Sale. Photo courtesy Denver Rotary Club.

Concurrent with the sale, volunteer Rotarians and DCIS students serve at the annual Pancake Breakfast in the cafeteria. "It's a great opportunity for everyone to work together," said 2007–2008 Denver Rotary President Doug Jackson, master chef at the Pancake Breakfast.

In 2010, the Peach Sale generated nearly $18,000, totaling approximately $92,000 in the past seven years. This amount is split equally between the Rotary International Foundation and the Denver Rotary Club Foundation.

Past and current Peach Chairs (left to right) Carol Duncan (a.k.a. Peach), Bryan Guice, Jay Yake (a.k.a. Pit), and Peach and Pit's daughter Ashley. Photo courtesy Denver Rotary Club.

DCIS students serve the annual Pancake Breakfast in 2008. Photo courtesy Denver Rotary Club.

Skip Ahern won the title "Peach King" three years in a row for selling the most peaches during the annual fundraiser. Photo courtesy Denver Rotary Club.

Peachy Pancake Flippers pose, left to right: Doug Jackson, Frank Lawrence, and Don Schlup. Photo courtesy Denver Rotary Club.

A 2006 World Community Service matching grant lead by Blair Gifford, provided school supplies for children in Piang Luang. Photo courtesy Denver Rotary Club.

Denver Rotary's World Community Service provided a matching grant to fund classroom equipment/supplies for the Al-Imtiaz Academy in Abbottabad, Pakistan. This project, led by Rotarian Ed Heath, was honored with a Rotary District Award in 2011. Photo courtesy Denver Rotary Club.

The proposals encompass a variety of causes, from dental relief in Ladakh, India, to South Africa Aids Education. Rotarian Ed Heath is currently involved with a school project in Abbottabad, Pakistan, for which Denver Rotary is the lead club, working with Rotary Clubs of Highlands Ranch, Mile Hi, Cherry Creek, Boulder, Granby, and District 5450.

The story of the Al-Imtiaz Academy began with Fatima Kulthum, a Pashtun girl prohibited from attending school because of strict social customs. Despite criticism, she learned to read and later risked social censure to send her daughter Imitiaz to the Punjab University, three hundred miles away. Inspired by her mother, Imtiaz Nawaz dedicated her life to teaching children who could not afford high-quality education. After several years of research, at age sixty-two she founded a nonprofit institution in a foothill city of Abbottabad in northeastern Pakistan.

"The Al-Imtiaz Academy opened in 1986 as a charitable school for young women," said Heath. "Their mission is to help kids from poor families, especially girls, although the school has since become coed. The Academy, which is operated by Pakistanis with families living in the United States, has been very successful. It now serves eleven hundred students with one hundred teachers. Their director of development, Ayesha Nawaz, is a former Rotary ambassadorial scholar to American University in Cairo, Egypt."

In 2009, the school received $31,246 for computer equipment, books, classroom furniture, and science lab equipment, with $18,000 allocated for a used school bus.

WORLD HEALTH FAIRS

In 1998, Denver Rotarian Grant Wilkins, U.S. Air Force Retired General Carl Riddell, and Steve Yoshida, past district governor of 5010 from the Homer-Kachemek Bay Club in Alaska, visited Russia at the request of RI President Jim Lacey. Yoshida wanted to expand the health fair program in their district, which included eastern Russia.

"After meeting with minister of health and others, we discovered that outside of St. Petersburg and Moscow, there was no organized health care," Wilkins recalled. "Everything collapsed when the Iron Curtain came down. Russia had full-blown epidemics of hypertension, AIDS, TB, diabetes—problems so enormous that local Rotary clubs could not make a dent."

Russian Rotary club members subsequently visited health fairs in Alaska. They also sent two Rotarians from Vladivostok, a medical doctor and an English professor, to witness Denver's 9Health Fair, the largest and oldest in the United States [Rotarian Jim Goddard is president and CEO of 9Health Fair]. The women visited two different sites every morning for a week. Inspired by what they saw, the Russians held their first health fair in 2000.

"Within a few years the district governor of Alaska had trained club presidents to hold these events in their own communities," Wilkins continued. "But we discovered that, although Russia now has about ninety clubs in the east, 80 percent of the population lives in the west. Russia has borders within borders—it actually crosses eleven time zones."

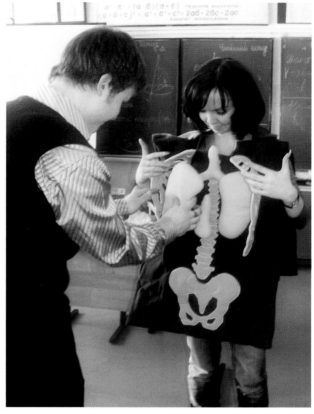

Russian Health Fair in action. Photo courtesy Denver Rotary Club.

The 9Health Fair in the Classroom Program (November 2009) was conducted at approximately sixty K–12 schools across the state. Denver Rotary's Top Gear New Member Class provided funding. Photo courtesy Denver Rotary Club.

151

Grant Wilkins receives the Open World Award on occasion of the program's tenth anniversary, September 29, 2009. Wilkins and Carolyn Jones initiated the program with the Library of Congress. Standing left to right: Senator Ted Stevens of Alaska; Grant Wilkins; Carolyn Jones, PDG District 5010 in Alaska, and RI's first woman trustee; James Billington, Librarian of Congress; and Ambassador John O'Keefe, executive director of the Open World Program. Photo courtesy Denver Rotary Club.

In 2002, Wilkins and Yoshida requested and received a 3-H grant (Health, Hunger, and Humanity) of $330,000 to help establish health fair centers in western Russia. Five years later, the RI Board of Directors recognized the World Health Fairs Action Group, which supports Rotarians who organize events featuring free screenings for treatable diseases and community education about health and wellness.

In 2009, a group of delegates visited Denver as part of the Library of Congress Open World Program to attend Health Fairs sponsored by Denver Rotary and five other clubs. Coordinator Irina Bulkley Hopkins told *The Rotarian* that the delegation represented "a broad variety of geographic territories in Russia where the demand for health fairs is higher due to remote locations and the impact of environmental pollution."

THE CITY AND THE FOUR-WAY TEST

Grant Wilkins likes to tell the story about Mayor (now Governor) John Hickenlooper's meeting with a group of delegates from the Library of Congress Open World Program in 2009.

"The mayor only had a few minutes to spend with us since he had to leave for another meeting," Wilkins recalled. "He talked about the city and some of the things we've done here. As he got ready to leave, someone mentioned that he hadn't said anything about Rotary."

Hickenlooper stood up, walked across the room and opened the closet door, where a banner hung, printed with a Rotary wheel. He pointed to the four-way test underneath:

Is it the TRUTH?
Is it FAIR to all concerned?
Will it build GOODWILL and BETTER
FRIENDSHIPS?
Will it be BENEFICIAL to all concerned?

The mayor told the group, "This is the way I govern the city, and this is the way I live my life."

Mayor John Hickenlooper shows Open World Program guests a banner printed with the Four-Way Test, which hung on a door in his office. Photo courtesy Denver Rotary Club.

Margaret Fomer, executive director of Denver Kids, Inc., accepts a faux check for $94,000 from Rotarian Perry Nissler on behalf of the Denver Rotary Club Foundation. Presumably, the real one was in the mail. Photo courtesy Denver Rotary Club.

"The U.S. government pays the air fare for this program," said Wilkins. "Any professionals—physicians, lawyers, even supreme court justices—spend ten days in Denver, stay in the homes of Rotarians and get together with people in their own professions. Each team has six members, four Russians, one facilitator, and an interpreter. In 2009, they sent five teams over at once. Besides visiting 9Health Fair sites, they also met with the governor and mayor."

Today, Health Fairs take place in China, which has two provisional clubs, Mexico, the Philippines, Mongolia and Fiji. "We're getting ready to go into Vietnam," Wilkins said. "This is a great program that benefits everyone. Denver Rotary and 9Health Fair can take much of the credit for getting it started."

SCHOLARSHIP PROGRAMS

In 1961, the Boys Work Committee was reorganized to include a College Scholarship Coordinating Committee. For many years, the Denver Broncos and Denver Rotary cosponsored an annual college scholarship for young people finishing high school. In the 1980s, the organizations contributed $15,000 and $7,500 respectively, to benefit recent high school graduates and students completing their education at colleges around the state. The renamed Denver Rotary Scholarship is now fully funded by the club.

A happy group of Denver Kids celebrating their graduation pose in a stairwell at the Denver Athletic Club. Photo courtesy Denver Rotary Club.

To support scholarship programs, Denver Rotary members originally made annual contributions to the Youth Development Fund. The Denver Rotary president would write a letter to members that would identify each member's share, which was approximately $100. In 1987–88, participation dropped from more than 90 percent in

In honor of longtime Denver Kids, Inc. Executive Director Donna Hultin's retirement, Denver Rotary established the Donna Hultin Excellence in Education Award. President Sue Fox (right) presented the first award on May 7, 2009 to Denver Kid and Rotary High School Scholarship recipient Corey Jacinto as Donna (center) proudly looks on. Photo courtesy Denver Rotary.

the 1970s to approximately 40 percent. Subsequently, the Denver Rotary Club Foundation took over responsibility for the youth programs.

Currently, the High School Scholarship and Achievement Awards provide approximately forty economically disadvantaged high school juniors/seniors with financial assistance ($55 to $75 a month) and Rotarian mentorship during the school year. A concurrent program, the college counseling initiative, offers college counseling to scholarship recipients, Denver Kids, and DCIS students.

Working with the Career Education Center at Denver Public Schools, the club also awards vocational scholarships based on need and merit, which allow students to continue their training at a college level. Rotarian Jim Mack initiated the vocational scholarship program.

Denver Rotary High School Scholarship Award recipients and Denver Kids graduates chat at the 2008 graduation program. Photo courtesy Denver Rotary Club.

Seeing double? Jim Mack, Denver Rotary president in 1999–2000, stands next to his portrait created by artist Robert Olson. For several years, Olson painted portraits of outgoing presidents. Photo courtesy Denver Rotary Club.

Denver Kids counselor Bobbe Hultin (far left) poses with 2008 graduate Jesse Quintana and her DKI mentor Elizabeth Hultin.. Photo courtesy Denver Rotary Club.

ERIC'S STORY

Through the High School Scholarship program (HSSAA), Rotarian Chuck Everill worked with a young student named Eric Ndikumane, a refugee from Burundi in Eastern Africa, one of the ten poorest nations in the world.

"Eric was the son of a small neighborhood general store–type merchant and his stay-at-home mom," Everill later wrote. "Both parents were children of farmers and neither went beyond sixth grade. Despite this, his father was quite successful. They had a car, and lived in a nice house in town. But tragedy struck when Eric was six and his dad was killed by soldiers during the Burundian Civil War. The chaos was everywhere, and Eric's mom decided to flee to the refugee camps in Tanzania. The family of ten, with children ranging from [ages] four to twenty-two, embarked on the laborious and frightening journey across war-torn Burundi. Two months later they arrived at the refugee camp, their home for the next five years. Eric attended a school, but there was no building, no desks, no books—just a teacher and a place to meet under a tree. After about three years, the family began applying for asylum. In a lottery-like process, they were assigned to Denver."

Eric was placed in sixth grade when he arrived in the United States. He knew no English and could barely read and write French. After only two years, his English language aquisition teachers informed the family that he was ready for all-English classes. By the time he reached high school, he was an honor student, still working hard to improve his English skills. To meet his goal—his lifelong dream of attending Stanford University—he had to achieve far more than the average student.

Through the High School Scholarship Program, Rotarian Chuck Everill worked with a young student named Eric Ndikumane, a refugee from Burundi in Eastern Africa, one of the ten poorest nations in the world. Photo courtesy Chuck Everill.

"I began working with Eric in September of 2006," Everill recalled. "It was clear that he was an outstanding young man. Eric and I worked on two major projects, exposing him to Stanford University and assisting with his application for the Gates Millennium Scholarship, one of the most prestigious and lucrative minority aid programs in North America."

Despite all Eric's hard work and Chuck's mentorship, Eric would not be accepted at Stanford. Putting aside the terrible disappointment, he persevered and went on to win the Gates Millennium Scholarship. He currently attends Columbia University, where he held a 3.3 grade average the first semester and a 3.6 for the second.

"For me, Eric's story speaks of the wonders of Rotary, and how the club offers to each of us fabulous opportunities for community service," Everill said. "It makes our lives so much richer and meaningful. I feel blessed by the assistance and opportunities I have received in my life, and I appreciate the Rotary programs that offer each of us a way to give back."

DENVER CENTER FOR INTERNATIONAL STUDIES

Denver Rotarian Dan Lutz founded the Denver Center for International Studies (DCIS) as a magnet program at West High School in 1985, while he

Students of the DCIS Interact Club traveled to Juarez, Mexico, in 2007 to help build houses. The club received the annual Interact Club of the Year award at the District Conference the following year. Photo courtesy Denver Rotary Club.

was the school principal. As part of Denver Rotary's Adopt-a-School Project to celebrate the Rotary International's Centennial, DCIS opened in 2006 in the former Baker Middle School (574 West Sixth Avenue) as a stand-alone magnet school. Currently enrolling 650 students, DCIS accepts youngsters in grades six to twelve and actively recruits at Denver Public Schools around the city through presentations to parents and children. Any student in the metro Denver area can apply.

"We end up with a diverse population," said Lutz. "About 50 percent of the kids come from a lower economic background. We enroll a large number of Latino and Asian students and we're trying to increase the number of African American kids." DCIS is opening a second school in the Montbello neighborhood.

The school offers courses in five languages and classes that emphasize international affairs, combining academics, intercultural interaction, and opportunities to travel and learn abroad. Students develop multilingual skills while participating in service activities at the school and on local, national, and international levels. Approximately 95 percent of DCIS graduates will attend some of the country's best colleges and receive financial aid awards from various entities.

"The program is designed to give students knowledge of public speaking, languages, and political and cultural dynamics," Lutz added. "We teach them how to apply what they learn in the context of problem solving on a worldwide scale. Kids learn that they can make a difference, and they're doing some pretty amazing things."

Club President Doug Jackson interviews 2007–2008 Youth Exchange student Gustav Forslid from Sweden at the annual DRCF Celebration Day. Photo courtesy Denver Rotary Club.

Lutz tells about one student, Tyler Quintana, who traveled to Sierra Leone on a medical project during his sophomore year. "He saw someone die because the village had no ambulance to take the patient to a hospital. As soon as he got home, he began a fundraising project directed by the Interact Club."

Two years later, with the help of the Rose Foundation, Project Cure (which is operated by Denver Rotarian Doug Jackson), and the Denver Rotary Club Foundation, the Interact Club is shipping the ambulance to Sierra Leone.

Denver Rotary activities with the school are channeled through the DCIS Interact Club, formed in 2005. Besides providing financial assistance, Club 31 works with schools to develop programs, provides mentorship, and invites students to attend regular Rotary meetings.

The club's very own Young "Old" Cho (far right) welcomes RI 2008–2009 President Dong-Kurn Lee from Seoul, Korea. Photo courtesy Denver Rotary Club.

Top Gear (2007) New Member Class President Eric White and his wife, Stephanie, prepare to hit a few balls at the annual golf tournament in 2009. Photo courtesy Denver Rotary Club.

To their delight, Denver Rotarian Peg Johnston and Bamidale Salam of Osuri State, Nigeria, ran into each other at the 2007 Rotary International Convention in Salt Lake City. Photo courtesy Denver Rotary Club.

MORE ROTARIANS TO REMEMBER

PETE SMYTHE
(Joined 1972. Classification: Author)

Former Denver Rotary president, 1981–1982, and one of the club's most active members, Pete Smythe was born in Glenn Rock, Wyoming, on July 10, 1912. A small

town gentleman with the heart of a cowboy, Smythe was a musician, composer, radio and TV personality, author, vocalist, band leader, and local celebrity. He became the first disc jockey in Denver when his show, *Meet the Boys in the Band*, aired on Radio Station KMYR in 1941. After spending much of the decade in Hollywood, he returned to Denver in 1948 to create the radio program, *The Pete Smythe General Store Show*, which aired

Members enjoyed watching entertainer and former club president Pete Smythe perform. Here, he is playing piano at a 1993 Presidents' Roundtable honoring the Outstanding Service Club project of the year. Photo courtesy Denver Rotary Club.

on TV from 1954 to 1969. He founded the imaginary town of East Tincup in 1951, standing on the platform "No taxes, No parking meters" and making himself mayor for life. Disguising his voice to create "hometown" characters like the old philosopher Moat Watkins ("Man who go through life looking for something soft is only going to find it under his head"), he regaled listeners with folksy stories and clever humor like a 1950s Garrison Keillor.

Often identified with the town of Golden, Smyth remained a familiar public figure for decades, honored by the National Western Stock Show as Citizen of the West in 1983. A man you could obviously trust, he became the original recorded voice passengers heard on Denver International Airport's train system and the Regional Transportation District's Light Rail. Although Smythe served on many boards, his heart was always with Denver Kids, Inc., which he promoted tirelessly. When he died on May 9, 2000, at age eighty-eight, the family requested that contributions be sent to that organization.

FRANK H. RICKETSON, JR.

(Joined 1945. Classification: Motion Pictures-Theaters)

Born October 22, 1895, in Leavenworth, Kansas, Ricketson worked as sports editor for *The Denver Post* in 1920, while finishing law school. Later a prominent public relations professional, he owned a chain of movie theaters and became president of the National Theaters chain. During the Depression, he and partner Charles Yeager created "Bank Night," a weekly drawing for cash prizes which rescued many movie theaters around the nation.

In the early 1930s, Ricketson joined in the effort to restore the Central City Opera House, luring top names in opera and theater to perform in the mountain community. As president and CEO of the Central City Opera Association from 1934 to 1956, he commissioned the original opera, *The Ballad of Baby Doe*, which focused national attention on Colorado and local history.

Ricketson was one of the founders of the Roundup Riders of the West and served on numerous boards, acting as a trustee of the University of Denver, Washington University, and the Denver Museum of Natural History, now the Denver Museum of Nature and Science. In 1980, he was named Citizen of the West by the National Western Stock Show. He died June 18, 1987, a lauded philanthropist and Rotarian admitted to the Colorado Business Hall of Fame in 1993. The Frank H. Ricketson Law Building at the University of Denver and the Ricketson Theater at the Denver Performing Arts Complex are named in his honor.

Frank Ricketson, Jr., one of the founders of the Roundup Riders of the West, was deeply involved with the effort to restore the Central City Opera House, luring top names in opera and theater to perform in the mountain community. Photo courtesy Denver Public Library Western History Department.

The wise emperor Marcus Aurelius Antonius maintained, "The true worth of a man is to be measured by the objects he pursues." Through this lens we can evaluate the real success of any given business.

—Doug Jackson, Denver Rotary President 2008–09

CHAPTER IX

Visions of Tomorrow

PRIORITIES FOR THE NEXT DECADE

Clean Water

An easily accessible source of clean water makes all the difference to the productivity of a community and the future of its children. During the next decade, many Denver Rotary world community service and regional projects will likely revolve around clean water.

"When I was chair of Health and Hunger Task Force 2002, the American Water Works Association [composed of all water suppliers in the United States] asked me to speak on Polio Plus at their annual convention," said Grant Wilkins. "After talking with their representatives (about 25 percent Rotarians), I discovered to my amazement that lack of clean water is even more lethal than polio, killings six thousand children every day. I went back to RI headquarters and urged that we put clean water up at the top of our priorities. At the time, none of us realized the enormity of what we were taking on.

Workers are building a dam at Vatusekiyasawa in Fiji, one of Denver Rotary's many water projects. Photo courtesy Denver Rotary Club.

Delighted children play with Doug Jackson, who was visiting the Campinas Brazil Hospital project. For this World Community Service project, Jackson's company, Project C.U.R.E., shipped a container of medical supplies to a children's cancer hospital in 2009. Photo courtesy Denver Rotary Club.

"The goal is to have all thirty-four thousand clubs do at least one clean water project," he added. "A few years ago, the Water and Sanitation Rotarian Action Group (WASRAG) formed solely to focus on water and sanitation. At any one time there are ten thousand water projects going around the world, from drilling wells to finding clean sources of water. By 2020 the United Nations plans to have at least a water supply and a latrine in every school in the world, including the Maasai, a settlement in East Africa with roaming tribes."

John Stewart, chair of the World Services Committee in 2009–2010 agreed that clean water has become the primary global objective for Rotarians. "Water is the lifeline in the daily struggle for survival in remote areas of the world," he said. "In many native villages, women have to walk several hours to a water source, which is often polluted. They have no time to do other work or plant gardens and the girls can't go to school. It's an incredible waste of time and energy and often a health hazard. The major thing we do is dig wells or teach the people how to purify the water they have, which might be contaminated with arsenic and lead. We contract out with engineering firms, and there's always a local host club and a great deal of Rotary involvement."

Rotarians gather for 2006 World Community Services Award Breakfast. Second Row, left to right: Peter van Dernoot, Lyn Sabichi, Roland Thornton, Phil Goedert, Doug Jackson, Joe Jensen, Hank Strauss, Ed Heath, Jim Nelson, and John Stewart. Front row: Young Cho, Grant Wilkins, Peg Johnston, Sue Fox, Bill Nelson, and Blair Gifford. Photo courtesy Denver Rotary Club.

One example is a slum in Nairobi Kenya called Kibera, where eight hundred thousand people live. "Denver Rotary is the lead club on the project," Stewart said. "It's sort of mind-blowing that nearly a million people, many from the countryside, have no clean water and no sewage treatment in the capital of a country. WASRAG has installed water kiosks, bathrooms, and showers, which are actually the first water structures in the area."

Les Garrison, 2008–09 World Services Committee chair, worked on a different kind of water project in the mountains of Guatemala. In 2005, Hurricane Stan hit the country's highland region, causing more than 650 deaths and destroying at least thirty-five thousand homes. The hurricane's heavy rains triggered immense mudslides as a half-mile river of mud rushed down the volcanic slopes at fifty m.p.h. above the town of Santiago Atitlán. When Panabáj, a community on the outskirts of the town, collapsed underneath the sludge, approximately 150 people lost their lives.

"The mud was fifty feet deep," said Garrison. "It wiped out all the pipelines, flooded the villages, and destroyed the crops." With the assistance of a 3-H Grant and PAVA, an aid program for highland communities, a four-year project reconstructed the water systems. According to Garrison, 70 percent of the construction went into building hand-washing stations.

Water projects like this hand-washing station in Guatemala are likely to be the focus of World Community Services efforts in the next decade. Photo courtesy Denver Rotary Club.

Club 31 cooperated with the Suva East Club in Fiji on a large "Water for Life" 3-H Grant that provided villagers in Fiji with clean, safe drinking water. Photo courtesy Denver Rotary Club.

Village youth celebrate the "Water for Life" grant in Fiji. Photo courtesy Denver Rotary.

EVERY STUDENT COUNTS. EVERY STUDENT GRADUATES.

Since Denver Rotary's fledgling years, the welfare of the city's youngsters has been a top priority. Through Denver Kids, Inc., which is still a primary beneficiary of Denver Rotary Club Foundation fundraising efforts, Club 31 continues to address "the forgotten children," those from disadvantaged backgrounds, left behind by an increasingly complex society and America's flawed system of education.

According to Glenna Norvelle, president/CEO of Denver Kids, Inc., participation by Denver Public School students has nearly doubled in the past five years. Recent statistics show that Denver Kids, Inc., has a 90 percent high school graduation rate, far above the DPS norm of 51.8 percent. The majority of graduating Denver Kids are the first in their families to finish high school. Approximately 88 percent pursue postsecondary education.

"Our program model obviously works, and this makes us a major resource for Denver Public Schools," said Norvelle. "Ultimately, we want to look at how we can have an even greater impact on the community."

Rotarian Brian Blankenburg plays tetherball with an unidentified youngster at the 2009 DCIS/Junior Achievement Team Teach Day at Greenlee Elementary. Photo courtesy Denver Rotary Club.

The organization plans to improve and expand the mentorship program and include more individuals from diverse backgrounds, the Spanish-speaking and individuals living in underrepresented neighborhoods. The Parent2Parent Program looks to achieve greater parental participation by giving parents an opportunity to

Rotarian Wynn Gandera and a DCIS student team-teach Junior Achievement. Photo courtesy Denver Rotary Club.

meet with experts (and one another) to discuss difficult or sensitive issues that students face in school, such as bullying. In January 2010, Denver Kids, Inc., launched their first electronic newsletter to share triumphs and provide updates to parents and the communities.

"A large part of our focus during the next few years will be strengthening foundational pieces," said Norvelle. "We're looking at strategic partnerships with organizations like Denver Active 20–30 Children's Foundation, a group of professional men ages twenty to thirty-nine who help at risk and disadvantaged children. They host an annual event, the Polo Classic, which raises hundreds of thousands of dollars for children's organizations, including ours."

High School Scholarship sponsors and their students relax at the annual Bowling Party at the DAC. Photo courtesy Denver Rotary Club.

Denver Kids, Inc., also works with groups such as Kroenke Sports (owners of Nuggets, Avalanche, Mammoth, and Rapids), which offers incentives to keep kids from skipping school. Recently, they provided sporting events tickets and Elitch Gardens passes to Denver Kids who attend all of their classes. Support from Club 31, however, has been the key to the program's success, both financially and through mentorship efforts.

"Denver Rotary has been our partner for decades," said Norvelle. "The club helped to give us our start and continues to connect us to the community in significant ways. Rotarians have made a huge contribution to our success."

CENTENNIAL PROJECT

To celebrate Denver Rotary's century of service to Colorado, Club President Roland Thornton (2009–2010) strongly encouraged the club to seek a project that would impart benefits well into the twenty-first century. The club finally settled on the effort to provide affordable and accessible broadband to school districts throughout the state.

Colorado currently ranks forty-second out of fifty states in broadband connectivity, with services costing ten times that of neighboring states. As a result, thousands of students, even along the Front Range, have inadequate access to High-speed Internet. School districts lack funding for escalating Internet prices, and private enterprise has no incentive to take on such a massive project, particularly in rural areas.

To address the problem, Colorado's Centennial Board of Cooperative Education (Centennial BOCES), a Longmont-based nonprofit providing services to a fourteen-member school district, proposed a public-private partnership, EAGLE-Net (Educational Access Gateway Learning Environment). The partnership would bring broadband, using primarily fiberoptic cable, to Colorado's 178 school districts and fifty-six community anchor institutions. The proposal gained support from major corporations, universities and organizations, including Cisco, IBM, Level 3 Communications, Colorado State University, and the Colorado Department of Transportation. Together they raised $34.7 million in cash and in-kind support and applied for federal government stimulus funding.

The new History Colorado Center is set to open in 2012. Photo courtesy VISIT DENVER: The Convention and Visitors Bureau.

"Their application was denied, but they were encouraged to reapply," said Grant Wilkins. "Apparently the one thing they lacked was evidence of broad-based community support."

Meanwhile, Denver Rotary had been looking into stimulus funding for a smaller Internet-related project. "Our original intent had been to team up with the new History Colorado Center to sponsor a distance learning center, so that K–12 students outside the Denver metro area could experience the History Colorado Center without a long bus ride," Wilkins said. "Recent studies have shown that students who learn history tend to excel in all subjects, and those who are well versed in their community's history become much better citizens."

The club's original plan was to provide direct communication with the History Colorado Center at about fifty locations around the state. "When we found that the EAGLE-Net connected many more areas, we got behind their project instead," said Wilkins. "They welcomed us with open arms."

The project gained media attention around Colorado, including a *Denver Business Journal* interview with EAGLE-Net CIO Denise Atkinson-Shorey and Centennial Year (2011–12) Club President Seth Patterson. Club 31 created an online petition, distributed a supportive bipartisan YouTube video featuring former Governor Richard Lamm and former Senator Hank Brown, made key phone calls and encouraged the involvement of school boards, elected officials and business groups.

In 2010, EAGLE-Net won a $100.6 million grant from the federal government to build out broadband infrastructure to 178 K–12 school districts, twenty-six libraries, fifteen community colleges, twelve BOCES, and three institutions of higher education. In all, the project will benefit approximately 830,000 K-12 public school students and 234 communities. At a September 13 press conference announcing the grant, a grateful Denise Atkinson-Shorey told Denver Rotarians, "We wouldn't be here without you!"

According to an article in *ICOSA* magazine (October–December 2010), "Soon Colorado Children will literally be able to operate an electronic microscope located at a distant research facility from their schoolroom in Meeker, Colorado, or control in real-time an astrophysical facility in Australia. The capacity and speed will be so great that literally every hospital, every library, every museum, every business, every government entity, and virtually every residence in the state will also be able to receive state-of-the-art Internet access."

EAGLE-Net will construct the "middle mile" portion of the high-speed Internet system. The "last mile" will connect the actual school buildings and classrooms. Hopefully, private enterprise will help to bridge that last mile. Leaders from Rotary District 5450 are meeting to discuss various ways to support the project in collaboration with Colorado Districts 5440 and 5470. By studying "best practices" in similar projects and facilitating discussions with rural, urban, and suburban communities, clubs throughout the state should discover multiple means and opportunities to champion the program.

Colorado Rotary leaders gather in January 2011 to discuss Colorado Rotary's High-Speed Internet Project. First row, left to right: Jim Halderman (District 5450 governor-elect); Mary McCambridge (District 5440 governor-elect); Kalyan Banerjee (Rotary International president-elect); Grant Wilkins (Rotary Club of Denver president, 1978–79; District 5450 governor, 1984–85; and a director of Rotary International, 1993–94); Harriet Downer (Rotary Club of Denver first vice president and High-Speed Internet Committee chair); and Mike Klingbiel (District 5450 governor-elect nominee). Back row: Karen Sekich, (District 5450 governor); Bryan Cooke (District 5440 governor); Lynn Hammond (Rotary Foundation trustee); Seth Patterson (Rotary Club of Denver president-elect); Doug McLemore (Rotary Club of Denver president); and Jim McGibney (Rotary Club of Denver president-elect-nominee). Other members of the committee are not pictured. Photo courtesy Denver Rotary Club.

ARTISTS OF THE WORLD®

Artists of America, a major fundraiser for the Denver Rotary Club Foundation for the preceding twenty years, had run its course by 2000. "Although we raised a significant amount of money, many expenses were involved," said Carolyn Smith, who chaired the committee in 1999 and 2000. "We took good care of the artists, produced a beautiful catalog, and spared nothing in marketing. Toward the end, the club wasn't making much of a profit. We were lucky to go out on a high, however, selling approximately $1.3 million worth of art in 2000. The following year the event would have been held during the week of 9-11."

Many members still wanted an arts event, however. "A group of us started meeting weekly about two years ago," said John Klug. "We knew we couldn't resurrect AOA because too much has changed in the past ten years. We live in an Internet-oriented world now, and art is sold very differently. Sotheby's of New York City and major art dealers and auctioneers now hang their art electronically. They have very sophisticated Websites for each auction."

DENVER ROTARY'S GOLDEN ANNIVERSARY MEMBERS

The City of Denver declared April 11, 2007, "Pete Thebus Day," in honor of his fifty-year perfect attendance membership in Denver Rotary. Left to right, back row: Club President Bill Houston and wife Jane, Pete Thebus and wife Peggy. Front row: District Governor Frank Sargent and wife Sherry. Photo courtesy Denver Rotary Club.

A new plan emerged for an event called Artists of the World (AOW), which would be an Internet-based international fundraiser.

"Through the Internet, we would display the work of artists in divergent and multiple genres," Klug said. "We would solicit participation from a limited number of Rotary Clubs in large cities around the world, such as Stockholm, London, Johannesburg, Tokyo, and Beijing. They would help us to acquire the best art in their region and help facilitate buyers. These clubs would receive a percentage of proceeds from any art they helped us acquire and sell, making it a fundraiser for them as well."

As planned, AOW would be billed as the finest and largest art show in the world, with all art juried, so that only very prominent artists can participate. If a smaller club acquires a piece of artwork, it can participate and receive a percentage of profits. Unlike AOA, which was a fixed priced sale, AOW is planned as an auction, a bid sale after the reserve is met.

The first show could come as early as May 2013. "We're talking to hotel chains that have worldwide operations and intercommunications like Four Seasons and

Rotarians who joined the club in 1961 are celebrating their Golden Anniversary during the club's centennial year. They are: Tom Hobson (February 16); Bob McWilliams (April 13), the club's oldest living past club president (1967–68); Bob Harry (May 18); and Dave Fleming (December 14), past club president (1987–88). Others who have recently celebrated fifty-plus years: Rex Post (August 5, 1952), Tupper Smith (July 5, 1953); Pete Thebus (April 11, 1957); Phil Pankey (May 1, 1958), and Art Starr (March 24, 1960). Peter Bowes, the youngest president in the club's history (1970–71), will observe his fiftieth year in 2013 (May 12, 1963). Pete Thebus, Phil Pankey, and Tom Hobson all have perfect attendance records. Pictured at right from top left clockwise are: Peter Bowes, Bob McWilliams, Rex Post, Tup Smith, Art Starr, Tom Hobson, Bob Harry, and Dave Fleming.

Phil Pankey (center) entertains guests at his fiftieth anniversary celebration. Photo courtesy Denver Rotary Club.

the Ritz," Klug said. "In major cities, for culmination night, the party will literally go around world. Some of the finest art pieces will be reserved for an international live auction that will be beamed electronically."

According to Grant Wilkins, the committee is seeking participation from Rotary International and some of the larger corporations and foundations worldwide. While the major portion of AOA proceeds went to Denver Kids, Inc., AOW profits are earmarked for clean water projects.

"This will be the next major effort," he said. "We're hoping to raise tens of millions of dollars for clean water, which would be funneled through Rotary or Rotary-related organizations. AOW could become one of the largest Rotary fundraisers in the world."

BRANCH RICKEY AWARD

The Branch Rickey Award, which has raised more than $1.5 million for the Denver Rotary Club Foundation over the past nineteen years, will continue as a key fundraiser for the club. According to Award founder and 2011 committee chair Jim Wilkins, the club has been seeking a national sponsor to take the event to a higher level. Denver Rotary recently hired a consultant to examine the possibilities. In 2010, with assistance from the Colorado Rockies owners, the committee made initial contact with Major League Baseball to obtain its endorsement. With national sponsorship and MLB approval, the award could generate proceeds in multiples of its current average.

"High profile sponsorship would attract attention through advertising, marketing, and a national brand," said Wilkins. "The future of the Branch Rickey Award is bright if current efforts are successful. Our consultant is confident that the award has tremendous value due to its twenty-year history and impressive list of recipients, many of whom are already enshrined in the Baseball Hall of Fame."

Rotarians and spouses enjoy a trip to Mesa Verde in 2008 as part of the club's "Discover Colorado" series. Photo courtesy Denver Rotary Club.

DENVER ROTARY TODAY

Darlene Mast, Denver Rotary's current executive director, has been called by grateful members, "the glue that holds the club together." Named "Rotarian of the Year" by Denver Kids, Inc., in 2010, Mast was chosen unanimously by the awards committee as "one of the most valuable and organized promoters Denver Kids could have."

Darlene first came to work for Rotary on July 6, 2004, to assist with an office management transition as her husband, Steve Mast, completed his term as president. She did such a fantastic job that the club officially hired her as executive director that October.

"The people are the best part of my job," she said. "I love working with the member volunteers, people who give back. Every president brings something new and different during their leadership, and both the club and I benefit."

Mast believes Denver Rotary needs to continue to bring quality younger members into the club and better identify how to plug them into Rotary. We have to learn to communicate in new ways, using different media." Currently, club and DRCF leaders are developing major campaigns to strengthen and increase both club membership and the corpus of the foundation.

The El Mariachi Juvenil de Bryant Webster Band performs for Denver Rotary at the December 17, 2010 Holiday Party. Photo courtesy Denver Rotary Club.

"People have only so many hours of free time in the day, and there are many charitable organizations out there that provide direct, hands-on volunteer opportunities. Denver Rotary is unique, however, because it offers one-stop shopping. As a large club, we can provide a variety of ways to serve. We present exceptional programs and speakers along with fellowship with like-minded leaders who want to make a difference."

One younger member, Gretchen Kneen, Board chair of Rocky Mountain Parents as Teachers, joined Denver Rotary in 2010. The daughter of Preston and Carolyn Smith, she recalls being introduced to the club as a child. Her favorite memories include trips with her parents to district and international Rotary meetings and watching Pete Smythe perform skits.

"Rotary was always such a big part of our lives," she said. "I think a lot of younger people don't quite understand what our club does, and how it's different from other groups. Once people come to a meeting, they see the power of Rotary and the complexity, and how the club connects with all the other Rotarians around the world. It's an amazing organization, but not everybody understands what we're all about. We need to get the word out."

LOOKING TOWARD TOMORROW

In December 2011, Denver Rotary Club 31 celebrates its Centennial Anniversary. After one hundred years of growth, club founder Gratton E. Hancock would hardly recognize the city but for the D&F Tower, the State Capitol, and perhaps the renovated Denver Dry Goods Building. Even so, it's likely that he would still feel at home at a club meeting, although the presence of women might

Rotarians Charlie Miller (right) and Jodi Brown (left) visit with a Chinese student at a CISEP (Collegiate International Student Engagement Program) event. The new initiative, chaired by Don Lewis, aims to build individual and Rotary-based relationships with international students. Approximately forty Club 31 TNT volunteers (the Nines and Tens, for classes 2009 and 2010) invite students to Rotary events, receptions, lunches and dinners, and sporting events, allowing plenty of time for individual attention and interpersonal communication. CISEP has extended to CU-Denver and the Colorado School of Mines, and similar programs are under development in the Boulder area.

come as surprise. As one of the early Rotary International directors, he undoubtedly would appreciate Denver Rotary's involvement with international humanitarian issues and the new projects that range far beyond the city's borders.

Shifting attitudes during the past one hundred years and an expanding global market have created a whole new Rotary dynamic. The club may have lost its direct pipeline to City Hall over the years, but Denver Rotary's support for the community continues through multiple avenues. Whether it's the National Western Stock Show, whose leaders and directors have historically been Denver Rotarians, or Denver Kids, Inc., and other youth-oriented programs, members of Rotary Club 31 have always worked hard and given generously to make the city a better place to live.

Some Denver Rotary traditions have disappeared over the decades while others have experienced only minor modifications. The Pledge of Allegiance still opens each meeting, although members are rarely called upon to stand up and sing. Luncheons move a little faster and business is conducted more briskly (and some might say, more efficiently), but there is still time for a handshake and a friendly chat. Celebrations like Stag Night and Ladies Night have faded away, but the Summer Picnics, the Holiday Parties and the spirit behind them have survived multiple generations. Behind it all, a sense of humor and loyal dedication to service still characterizes a Denver Rotarian.

The 2009 Himalayan Dental Relief Project, a WCS matching grant lead by Rotarians Frank King and John Stewart, brought dental volunteers overseas to provide first-time dental care to children in need. Photo courtesy Denver Rotary.

The World Community Service Committee participated in a matching grant project that supplied furniture, computers, books, play field restoration, and painting of classrooms for the Puebla Day Care Center in Mexico. Photo courtesy Denver Rotary Club.

"The club means different things to different people," said Carl Lindsay. "For some, it's all about Denver Kids, while others think that World Community Service Projects take priority. Many join for the social interaction, fellowship, and the opportunity to achieve a common goal or gain a voice in local affairs. The younger crowd has their own interests and priorities, as do those who have been members for decades. If there's a common denominator, I imagine it goes back to the concept of 'Service Above Self' and the commitment to work together, support each other, and help others."

Children at a Kenya orphanage benefited from a World Community Service matching grant lead by Rotarian Kemp Will, which provided a sustainable vegetable growing program to support street orphans in Meru and a school in Nairobi. Photo courtesy Denver Rotary Club.

"At the heart of Rotary is the collective energy of so many fine people who function in this large club somewhat independently," said Club President Doug McLemore (2010-2011). "It may be through a committee, a project, a task—with a student, by a vase of flowers, a thank you card, a single smile. It's that sense of individual drive that leads members to find their own piece of the Rotary pie. Sometimes they're swept up in a large project, sometimes they shine just by themselves by working with one student. Both are courageous and honorable."

Members of Denver Rotary Club 31 can be proud of their heritage and their incredible accomplishments over the past century. A new generation with different priorities will undoubtedly make their own way in the future, and that is as it should be. But in the end, it's that sense of commitment and pride in the city, each other and Rotarians worldwide that will lead the club through the next one hundred years.

To see where you are going, Denver Rotarians, just take a look at where you've been.

Rotarians Jean Herman and Karl Berg (right to left) enjoy the Scholastic Arts Award exhibition at the Denver Art Museum in February 2011. Photo courtesy Denver Rotary Club.

Rotarians (left to right) Pete Thebus, Dick Metcalfe, Sue Fox, and Holly McLemore volunteer at the 9Health Fair in April 2011. Photo courtesy Denver Rotary Club.

Marlene Wilkins immunizes an infant on Rotary National Immunization Day. Photo courtesy of Grant Wilkins.

Denver area Rotarians gather for the lighting of the End Polio Now at the City and County Building on February 23, 2011. Photo courtesy of David Talbot.

Youngsters from the 9Health Fair Health in the Classroom program show their appreciation to Denver Rotary. Denver Rotary's Top Gear 2007 New Member Class partially funded the program. Photo courtesy Denver Rotary Club.

ROTARIANS WHO MAKE A DIFFERENCE

GRANT WILKINS
(Joined 1969. Classification: Highway Advertising)

Grant Wilkins is appreciated worldwide for his dedicated service to Denver Rotary and Rotary International. Photo courtesy Denver Rotary Club.

Grant Wilkins' accomplishments in Denver Rotary are numerous and legendary. Growing up in a family of Rotarians, he was inspired by his father, who belonged to five different Rotary clubs in four states. During the past forty-odd years, Grant Wilkins has been president of Denver Rotary in 1978–79, governor of District 5450 in 1984–85, and a director of Rotary International in 1993–94. He served on the RI Finance Committee, which he chaired for a year, on the original U.S.C. B. Polio Plus Committee, as consultant to the RI Foundation, and as the RI president's representative to numerous district conferences around the world. A founder of Artists of America, a fundraiser that earned $1,894,032 for the Rotary Club Foundation during its 20-year history, Grant has been active in the Polio Plus campaign since its conception. He and his wife, Marlene (also a Denver Rotarian), represented RI at a National Immunization Day in the Ivory Coast, which they termed "a life-changing experience."

Wilkins has served on multiple RI committees worldwide and as Rotary's representative to the Library of Congress in the formation of the Russian Leadership program, now called the Open World. He was voted District 5450 Rotarian of the Year in 1995, and in 2009 received the RI "Service Above Self" Award, given to only 150 Rotarians in the world in any given year. He has received several other honors, including the Rotary Foundation Award for Distinguished Service and the International Service Award for a Polio-Free World.

Grant spent the majority of his business life as CEO and owner of Mountain States Advertising. Now retired, he and Marlene enjoy traveling and collecting Native American Art.

JIM WILKINS
(Joined 1978. Classification: Sales Management; Current: Real Estate-Agency)

Jim Wilkins poses with his Four Avenues of Service citation. Photo courtesy Denver Rotary Club.

A second-generation Rotarian like his brother, Grant, Jim Wilkins has served as club president in 1994–95 and Denver Rotary Club Foundation president in 2003–04. He has been voted Denver Rotary's Rotarian of the Year in 1999–2000, Denver Kids' Rotarian of the Year in 2005, and winner of the District 5450 Governor's Discretionary Award in 2005.

In 1991, Wilkins founded the Branch Rickey Award, Denver Rotary's chief fundraiser. He has served on or chaired innumerable committees, including the World Community Services Committee (both Denver Rotary and District 5450), the Peach Sale Committee, and the Grants Committee. Wilkins has been a fundraiser, a Board member, and a mentor for Denver Kids, Inc.

Along with Denver Rotary activities, Wilkins also has served as Capital Campaign chair for the Griffith Center for Children, sponsored by the Emily Griffith Opportunity School. He has been a trustee for Hastings College in Nebraska, recognized as one of the finest liberal arts colleges in the country. An avid local history buff, Wilkins has been Board member, vice chair, chair, and docent trainer at Four Mile Historic Park, an organization in which he remains active.

Although he retired in 1995, Jim Wilkins still leaves the house at 7 a.m. and gets home about 5 p.m. His typical day is a minimum of three meetings and a maximum of six. "I don't do anything I don't want to do," he said. "My passion is nonprofits. My passion is kids who need help."

WILLIAM H. (BILL) HORNBY

(Joined 1966. Classification: Newspaper Publishing)

Born in Kalispell, Montana, on July 14, 1923, Bill Hornby graduated from Stanford University in 1944, received his M.A. in journalism in 1947 and later did postgraduate study at the London School of Economics. He worked for the *San Francisco News, Associated Press,* and *Great Falls Montana Tribune* before joining *The Denver Post* in 1957 as a copyreader.

Bill worked his way up to managing editor at the *Post,* became executive editor in 1970 and vice president in 1972. He also served as president of the Colorado Historical Society, American Society of Newspaper Editors, Denver Rotary Club 31 in 1976–77, first Denver Rotary Foundation president in 1977–78, and later a trustee and governor of Rotary International District 5450 in 1988–89. A staunch supporter of First Amendment rights during disputes in the 1970s, Bill helped spur editorials and news stories in more than fifty newspapers throughout the country. As board chair of the Colorado Historical Society, he worked tirelessly for historic preservation with his late wife, former director Barbara Sudler Hornby.

Bill Hornby's dedicated service to the club is ongoing. He and Denver Post editor Palmer Hoyt kept Rotary activities in the news for decades. Photo courtesy Denver Rotary Club.

A dedicated Rotarian, Hornby wrote frequently about Club 31 in the *The Denver Post* and kept the club posted on the city's newspapers and their role in the community. While Denver Rotary Club president, he penned *A Club and a City* for the Denver Rotary's Seventy-fifth Anniversary Celebration in 1986, publishing the book through his own efforts. He also wrote an update covering the years 1987 through 1991.

Along with Denver Rotary, Hornby also attends Rotary Club of Englewood with his wife, Suzanne Davis Hornby. Suzanne's grandfather, Harry Ruggles, served as Rotary's fifth original member in 1905. According to Suzanne, he initiated community singing at Rotary, a tradition that continues in many clubs. Together, Bill and Suzanne are still active in club projects.

ARMIN P. (PETE) THEBUS, JR.

(Joined 1957. Classification: Produce Wholesaling)

A walking history of Denver Rotary Club 31, Pete Thebus can claim perfect attendance at weekly Denver Rotary meetings since he joined the club on April 11, 1957. Thebus came from a long line of Rotarians, since his grandfather, Fred Andrews, and uncle, John Thebus, were both longtime members of the club.

At age twenty-nine, Pete Thebus became president and owner of the Green Brothers Fruit and Produce Company. He served as a Denver Rotary Club Board member from 1972 to 1974 and as the club's sergeant-at-arms from 1961 to 1992. Pete Thebus has been famous for greeting generations of Rotarians at the door—by name! His remarkable memory for names and faces has long astonished his delighted colleagues, especially when the club had nearly six hundred members. A Paul Harris Fellow and a Denver Rotary Club Foundation Fellow, he is a past recipient of the Denver Kids, Inc., Rotarian of the Year Award. His support and commitment to the goals and programs of Rotary International and Denver Rotary Club led the City and County of Denver to proclaim Pete Thebus Day on April 11, 2007.

Pete Thebus, longtime sergeant-at-arms for the club, has an incredible memory for faces. Seen here in the 1980s, he greets Roland Boner (left) and Monte Pascoe. Photo courtesy Denver Rotary Club.

THE DENVER ROTARY CLUB FOUNDATION PRESIDENTS

John R. Dickinson	1978–79
Kenneth W. Caughey	1979–80
H. Preston Smith*	1980–83
Roger L. Kinney*	1983–85
William C. Kurtz*	1985–87
William F. Beattie*	1987–89
Richard D. Heiserman	1989–90
Joseph B. Blake	1990–93
Judy Wagner	1993–94
Richard W. Metcalfe	1994–95
C. Wills Long	1995–96
James C. Mack	1996–97
Richard E. Reuss	1997–98
Brooke B. Leer	1998–99
Linda S. Tafoya	1999–00
Robert M. Hurley	2000–01
Clark E. Ewald	2001–02
George I. Ahern	2002–03
James M. Wilkins	2003–04
Rike D. Wootten	2004–05
Peter J. Wall	2005–06
Anna Maria Larsen	2006–07
Donald J. Best, Jr.	2007–08
Charles H. Everill	2008–09
Charles I. Thompson	2009–10
Frank D. Lawrence	2010–11
Debra L. DeMuth	2011–12

Multiple terms

THE ROTARY CLUB OF DENVER ROTARIANS OF THE YEAR

Michael Muftic	1998–99
Jim Wilkins	1999–00
Carolyn Smith	2000–01
Francisco & Lyn Sabichi	2001–02
Pete Wall	2002–03
Bill Nelson	2003–04
Donna Hultin	2004–05
Jim Mack	2005–06
Peg Johnston	2006–07
Doug McLemore	2007–08
Grant Wilkins	2008–09
Dennis Kuper	2009–10
John Klug	2010–11

THE ROTARY CLUB OF DENVER NEW ROTARIANS OF THE YEAR

Karl Konrad	2002
Chris Chew	2003
Irina Bulkley-Hopkins	2004
Matt Morehead	2005
Seth Patterson	2006
Harriet Downer	2007
Carol Duncan & Jay Yake	2008
Jim Johnston	2009
Jodi Brown	2009
Bryan Hickel	2011

DENVER KIDS, INC. ROTARIANS OF THE YEAR

Ed Small	2004
Jim Wilkins	2005
Pete Wall	2006
Pete Thebus	2007
Denny O'Brien	2008
Francisco & Lyn Sabichi	2009
Darlene Mast	2010
Charlie Miller	2011

MEMBERSHIP ROSTER BY SENIORITY

(as of 9/1/11)

8/5/52	Rex Post	1/17/80	Gale Daniel	7/9/89	Evelyn Hottenstein
5/7/53	Tup Smith	1/17/80	Joe Jensen	10/8/89	Dianna Kunz
4/11/57	Pete Thebus	2/28/80	Jeff Pryor	10/8/89	Dennis Kuper
5/1/58	Phil Pankey	4/24/80	Larry Bohning	1/3/90	Jim Cohig
3/24/60	Art Starr	8/14/80	Bill Houston	4/19/90	Rick Bowman
2/16/61	Tom Hobson	8/14/80	Dick Metcalfe	7/6/90	Nick Muller
4/13/61	Bob McWilliams	8/28/80	Clem Mulder	8/16/90	Jim Johnson
5/18/61	Bob Harry	11/6/80	Len Johnson	11/1/90	Wellington Webb
12/14/61	Dave Fleming	11/12/80	Les Larsen	12/13/90	Bud Figel
5/12/63	Peter Bowes	3/19/81	Hugh Brown	5/30/91	Fred Davine
8/6/64	Bob Sawyer	5/3/81	Tom Vincent	7/3/91	Jim McGibney
2/25/65	Rike Wootten	8/13/81	Steve Foster	9/26/91	Robin Wise
3/25/65	Roger Kinney	12/3/81	Francisco Sabichi	1/16/92	Fred Grover
6/18/65	Howard Kast	2/12/82	Bob Thompson	4/23/92	Dean Laudeman
3/25/66	Dick Deane	4/22/82	Steve Mast	7/30/92	Barbara Berv
3/25/66	Bill Hornby	8/7/82	Jim Woodward	12/11/92	Stephen Block
1/19/67	Jim McFall	12/16/82	Tom Rogers	1/7/93	Dougal McDougal
1/16/69	Bob Timothy	6/10/83	Blaine Chase	3/6/93	Harry Ellison
2/1/69	Grant Wilkins	9/15/83	Wills Long	3/18/93	John Willson
8/21/69	Bill Kugler	11/15/83	Tom Craine	4/3/93	Peg Johnston
7/20/70	Mark Murray	1/19/84	Phil Heinschel	4/11/93	Phil Goedert
11/19/70	Jim White	5/24/84	Ted Friedman	7/1/93	Pete Jenkins
2/25/71	Jim Warner	7/6/84	R.J. Ross	9/12/93	Sue Anschutz-Rodgers
4/18/71	Marlin Weaver	8/11/84	Duane Bucher	9/12/93	Sid Brooks
5/13/71	Dick Koeppe	8/23/84	Harley Shaver	9/30/93	Bob Kapelke
9/24/71	Alan White	9/2/84	Jack Barker	11/11/93	Bruce Wagner
2/6/72	Blair Kittleson	9/13/84	Arnie Goldblatt	12/16/93	Sandy Adams
7/9/72	Bob Harris	2/21/85	Dale Harris	1/13/94	Steve Tucker
2/8/73	Seymour Simmons	6/20/85	Jerry Middel	3/11/94	Larry Gloss
3/5/73	Kerm Darkey	7/3/85	Jim Mack	5/26/94	John Baker
5/24/73	Frank King	9/19/85	Dick Harvey	6/16/94	Chuck Turner
7/19/73	Ed Small	9/26/85	Carl Lindsay	9/15/94	John Klug
8/3/73	Joe Blake	2/27/86	Karl Berg	10/11/94	Michael Muftic
12/14/73	Bill Diss	4/9/86	Pete Wall	10/13/94	Tucker Trautman
4/25/74	Fred Taylor	10/2/86	Skip Ahern	1/3/95	Stan Dempsey
10/10/74	Bev Hutter	10/23/86	Steve Close	1/12/95	David Lee
2/14/75	Mario Mapelli	4/16/87	Don Kany	2/2/95	Jane Withers
10/30/75	Bill Aragon	5/3/87	Todd Bacon	5/25/95	Mike Shaw
2/11/76	Roy Berkeley	5/14/87	Rod Greiner	7/9/95	Peter van Dernoot
5/8/76	Steve Connor	6/18/87	Mike O'Connell	7/12/95	Greg Osborn
9/12/76	Joe Wagner	9/24/87	Jean Jones	8/24/95	Mark Boulding
10/21/76	Gerry Quiat	10/9/87	Young Cho	9/14/95	Steve Duree
1/13/77	Bill Slifer	1/12/88	Carolyn Smith	9/21/95	Johnny Hsu
1/20/77	Giff Eckhout	2/18/88	Frank Lawrence	9/21/95	Wayne Schell
4/21/77	John Lucken	5/5/88	Bill Johnson	10/26/95	Fred Diss
5/5/77	Jim Wilkins	5/12/88	Bruce Peterson	10/26/95	Felicia Muftic
8/18/77	Stu Moore	6/9/88	Joe Hodges	1/2/96	Marilyn Renninger
1/19/78	Chuck Pell	8/25/88	Lee Everding	3/14/96	Charlie Miller
7/20/78	El Berger	8/25/88	Stephanie Foote	5/16/96	Al Timothy
12/10/78	Ved Nanda	10/13/88	Hank Strauss	10/15/96	Sherry Helmstaedter
5/7/79	La Voy Robison	1/19/89	Tom Woodruff	10/15/96	Les Volpe
5/17/79	Chuck Thompson	4/5/89	Harry Arkin	12/17/96	Dave Dennis
9/6/79	Kent Winker	6/22/89	Chuck Everill	1/21/97	Earl Wright

5/20/97	Lyn Sabichi	
11/18/97	Doug Jackson	
1/20/98	Don Schlup	
3/17/98	Becky Mallory	
3/17/98	Adams Price	
4/20/99	Jim Nelson	
4/20/99	John Stewart	
11/16/99	Andre van Hall	
3/21/00	Mike Severns	
8/15/00	George Sissel	
1/16/01	Sue Fox	
3/20/01	Alan Friedberg	
3/20/01	Jeff Haughton	
4/17/01	Rob Clinton	
4/17/01	Russ Haskell	
4/17/01	Su Ryden	
4/17/01	David Sprague	
4/17/01	Lee White	
4/17/01	Martin Wohnlich	
5/15/01	Les Lee	
7/19/01	Debbie DeMuth	
7/19/01	Ed Heath	
10/16/01	Donna Hultin	
12/18/01	Ron Zimmermann	
2/14/02	Bryan Guice	
2/14/02	Art Roy	
9/17/02	Jean Herman	
10/15/02	Mark Clouatre	
10/15/02	Rich Spong	
11/19/02	Wick Rowland	
12/17/02	Branch Rickey	
5/28/03	Jack Green	
7/15/03	Lyn Woods	
8/19/03	Ted Trask	
10/21/03	Lucius Ashby	
11/18/03	Ed Crabtree	
11/19/03	Chris Harr	
12/19/03	Dave Benson	
12/19/03	Alice Bullwinkle	
1/20/04	Roland Thornton	
2/19/04	John Hickenlooper	
4/20/04	Les Garrison	
6/15/04	Alison Clark-Hardesty	
7/20/04	Peter Tedstrom	
12/21/04	Tony Leuthold	
1/18/05	Seth Patterson	
2/15/05	Paul Fischer	
3/16/05	Rich Harris	
3/16/05	John Nelson	
7/19/05	Dan Lutz	
8/16/05	Mike Jaster	
11/15/05	Scott White	
12/20/05	Mike Miller	
2/21/06	Doug McLemore	
3/23/06	Terry Kenyon	
4/18/06	Warren Donder	
5/16/06	Kristi Shaffer	
6/21/06	Aaron Hughes	
9/19/06	Bill Korstad	
11/21/06	Harriet Downer	
11/21/06	Jim Marlow	
12/19/06	Kise La Montagne	
2/20/07	Brian Blankenburg	
2/20/07	Bill Ritter	
2/20/07	Kelly Walker	
3/20/07	Jim Goddard	
4/17/07	Garry Lawrenz	
5/15/07	Carol Duncan	
5/15/07	Jay Yake	
7/17/07	Sandy Purcell	
7/17/07	Tim Sheahan	
7/17/07	Will Snider	
8/21/07	Bob Lowdermilk	
9/18/07	Nancy Austin	
9/18/07	Brooke Schiffner	
9/18/07	Eric White	
11/20/07	Phil DeVargas	
12/18/07	Cindy Myers	
12/19/07	Wynn Gandera	
1/17/08	Melissa Kelley	
2/19/08	Ron McOmber	
3/18/08	Jim Johnston	
3/18/08	Craig Mills	
3/31/08	Kevin Seggelke	
4/15/08	Mitch Benedict	
5/20/08	Susan Brushaber	
5/20/08	Tom Butler	
5/20/08	Randy Kenworthy	
5/20/08	Gary Schrenk	
5/22/08	Gene Wiggs	
6/24/08	Bob Coombe	
6/30/08	Sue Davis Hornby	
7/15/08	Darlene Mast	
8/19/08	Daren Forbes	
9/16/08	Bob Heiserman	
9/16/08	Glenna Norvelle	
10/21/08	Steve Riley	
11/18/08	David Trickett	
12/16/08	Bob Morehead	
12/16/08	Stephen Parce	
1/20/09	J. D. Dreyer	
1/20/09	Ken Hubbard	
2/17/09	Jane Barnes	
2/17/09	Bruce Fowler	
4/21/09	Pat Lewis	
5/17/09	Giles Poulson	
5/19/09	Ed Nichols	
5/19/09	Marlene Wilkins	
6/16/09	John Finegan	
6/16/09	Debby Kaufman	
7/21/09	Jodi Brown	
9/15/09	Karyn Katsenes	
9/15/09	Bob Palmer	
9/15/09	Pierre Powell	
10/20/09	Dave French	
10/20/09	Jeff Howard	
10/20/09	Don Lewis	
11/17/09	Joe Wicentowich	
11/18/09	Karli Anderson	
12/15/09	Lauren Lehman	
12/15/09	Kemp Will	
1/19/10	Mike Dent	
2/16/10	Kristin Candella	
2/16/10	Bob Hardaway	
2/16/10	Gretchen Kneen	
3/16/10	Dave Mariea	
5/18/10	Jim Brendel	
5/18/10	Gwen Shuster-Haynes	
6/15/10	Pam Adams	
6/15/10	Synthia Baumer	
6/15/10	Steve Brownson	
6/15/10	Bill Chrismer	
6/15/10	Lynn Dawson	
6/15/10	Chad McDonnell	
6/15/10	Sundru Moodley	
6/15/10	Doug Pogge	
6/15/10	Victor Porak de Varna	
6/29/10	Becky Takeda-Tinker	
6/29/10	Steven Zoncki	
7/20/10	Kelly Brough	
7/20/10	Denise Brown	
7/20/10	Kari Koppes	
7/20/10	Jon Lorenz	
7/20/10	Holly McLemore	
7/20/10	Alex Porter	
7/20/10	Kris Walker	
8/17/10	Bryan Hickel	
9/21/10	Larry Wiberg	
10/19/10	Tom Base	
11/16/10	Joe Miller	
11/16/10	Billy Wynne	
2/15/11	Paul Andrews	
2/15/11	Matt Jordan	
2/15/11	Kurt Pletcher	
2/15/11	Carter Sales	
2/15/11	Tim Scott	
3/15/11	Mark Flynn	
3/15/11	Virgil Scott	
4/19/11	Nick LeMasters	
5/17/11	Valerie Hopkins	
5/17/11	Maria Puzziferro	
6/21/11	Lauren Evans	
6/21/11	Stewart Gallagher	
6/21/11	Luke Hartley	
6/21/11	Todd Krapf	
7/19/11	Diana DeGette	
7/19/11	Bob Green	
7/19/11	Michael Hancock	
7/19/11	Ron Sherbert	
7/19/11	Rusty Wilkins	

SOURCES

INTERVIEWS

Berg, Karl

Bowes, Peter

Davis, Sue

Emmons, Charles

Everding, Lee Harding

Everill, Chuck

Fox, Sue

Garrison, Les

Grover, Breck

Heath, Ed

Hornby, Bill

Hultin, Donna

Jackson, Doug

Jones, Jean

Kinney, Roger

Klug, John

Lindsay, Carl

Lutz, Dan

Mast, Darlene

McFall, Jim

McLemore, Doug

Moore, Stu

Norvelle, Glenna

O'Connell, Mike

Sabichi, Francisco

Sabichi, Lyn

Smith, Carolyn

Smith, Tup

Stewart, John

Strauss, Hank

Thebus, Pete

Villereal, Luis

Wall, Pete

Weeams, Claricy

Wilkins, Grant

Wilkins, Jim

White, Jim

Yake, Jay

Past Denver Rotary Foundation Presidents' and Trustees Meeting, December 17, 2010: Jim Wilkins, Rike Wootten, Charlie Miller, Debbie DeMuth, Pete Wall, Charles Everill, and Frank Lawrence.

Past Denver Rotary Presidents' Meeting, December 17, 2010: Steve Mast, Mike O'Connell, Roland Thornton, P. Douglas McLemore, Susan Fox, Bill Houston, Jim Mack, Tom Rogers, and Bob Kapelke.

BOOKS

America's Switzerland, Estes Park and Rocky Mountain National Park, the Growth Years. James Pickering, University Press of Colorado, Boulder, CO. (2005).

The Beast. Judge Ben B. Lindsey and Harvey O'Higgins. Doubleday, Page and Co., Garden City, NY (1911).

A Century of Service, the Story of Rotary International. David C. Forward. Rotary International, Evanston, IL (2003).

A Club and a City: Rotary Club of Denver 1911–1986. Bill Hornby. Denver Rotary Club 31, Denver (1986).

Colorado Pioneers in Picture and Story. Alice Polk Hill. Heritage Books Inc., 1915.

History of Colorado, Vol. 1. Edited by Wilbur Fisk Stone, S. J. Clarke Publishing Co. Chicago, IL (1918).

Church Publicity, the Modern Way to Compel Them to Come In. Dr. Christian Reisner. University of Wisconsin, Milwaukee, WI (1913).

Denver Metro, A Millenium Celebration. Sonia Weiss. Heritage Media Corp. Dallas, TX (2000).

Denver—Mining Camp to Metropolis. Stephen J. Leonard and Thomas J. Noel. University Press of Colorado, Boulder, CO (1990).

Denver—The City Beautiful and Its Architects 1893–1941. Barbara S. Norgren and Thomas J. Noel. Historic Denver, Inc. Denver (1987).

Denver Tramway Strike of 1920. Augustine Ryan, Edward Thomas and John Divine. Commission on the Church and Social Service. New York, NY (1922).

Colorado, a History of the Centennial State. Carl Abbott, Stephen J. Leonard, Thomas J. Noel. University Press of Colorado, Boulder, CO (2005).

Mile High Tourism, Denver's Convention and Visitor History. Thomas J. Noel and Debra B. Faulkner. Visit Denver and Center for Colorado and the West. Denver (2010).

Places around the Bases. Diane Bakke and Jackie Davis. Westcliffe Publishers, Englewood, CO (1995).

The Queen City, A History of Denver. Lyle W. Dorsett and Michael McCarthy, Second Edition, Pruett Publishing Co. Boulder, CO (1976).

Robert Speer's Denver, The Mile High City in the Progressive Era, 1904–1920. Phil Goodstein, New Social Publications. Denver. (2004).

Sacred Stones, Colorado's Red Rocks Park and Amphitheater. Thomas J. Noel. Denver's Division of Theaters and Arenas. Denver (2004).

Thunder in the Rockies, The Incredible Denver Post. Bill Hosakawa. William Morris & Co. New York, NY (1976).

Trials and Triumphs: A Colorado Portrait of the Great Depression with FSA Photographs. Stephen J. Leonard. University Press of Colorado, Boulder, CO (1993).

NEWSPAPERS

The Denver Business Journal
The Denver Post
The Denver Times
The New York Times
The Rocky Mountain News
The Syracuse Herald

MAGAZINES AND PUBLICATIONS

Denver Chamber of Commerce Bulletin, 1912
Denver Rotary Newsletters/Programs, 1925–1941
ICOSA, October–December 2010
Mile High Keyway, 1941–2011
Municipal Facts Monthly, 1912–1916
The Colorado Lawyer, July 2003
The Rotarian, 1911–2011

CORRESPONDENCE

Letters from Paul Harris and Chesley A. Perry to Gratton E. Hancock, 1911–1912.

Letter to Congress, June 13, 1926. Signed by various public figures, including Rotarians, who supported U.S. participation in the Hague World Court.

Letter of concern, December 1928, signed by Rotarians working legislation regarding Rocky Mountain National Park legislation.

Letter of appreciation to Denver Rotary, Ralph D. Potter, February 10, 1991.

OTHER DOCUMENTS

Annual Rotary Stag Night program, April 28, 1927.

Water and Arid Lands of the Western United States. World Resources Institute Study by Mohamed T. El-Ashry.

Denver Rotary Membership Rosters through 2011.

Various Denver Rotary Club, Denver Rotary Club Foundation and Denver Kids Annual Reports through 2011–12.

Various Denver Rotary Club historical documents.

WEBSITES

Ancestry.com. (Gratton E. Hancock, Charles Franklin, Sam Dutton)

American Municipal Pipe Organ Web site, www.municipalorgans.net

City of Denver, www.denvergov.org (City Auditor Dennis Gallagher)

Project C.U.R.E., www.projectcure.org

Rotary District 5450, www.rotary5450.org

Rotary Club of Denver, www.denverrotary.org

PHOTO CONTRIBUTIONS

Karl Berg

Roy Berkeley

Rosemary Fetter

Barbara Knight

Bob Lowdermilk

Carolyn Smith

David Talbot

Jim White

Grant Wilkins

Rike Wootten

Auraria Higher Education Center

Denver Public Library Western History Department

Denver Rotary Archives

History Colorado

Rotary International Archives

Visit Denver, Convention & Visitors Bureau

ACKNOWLEDGMENTS

I want to thank all members of Denver Rotary Club 31 who participated in the creation of this book and helped to ensure its accuracy. Particular credit goes to project manager Carl Lindsay, whose dedicated involvement, attention to detail, and perseverance kept us all on track. This book could not have been completed without his efforts.

I also want to thank Denver Rotary Executive Director Darlene Mast, who provided invaluable assistance and information. Carl Lindsay and Roy Berkeley initiated the project, and Grant Wilkins spent hours in multiple interviews. Administrative Assistant Jamie Demmitt and Roy Berkeley helped with images, while Pete Thebus identified many individuals in older photos. Cathleen Norman of Donning Company Publishers always made herself available to answer questions and keep the project moving, and CU-Denver graduate student Abby Fisher Hoffman assisted with research during the book's early stages, Breck Grover served as a necessary link to the mayor's and governor's offices. Artist Barbara Froula, former Rotary Ambassadorial Scholar, provided beautiful cover art.

Additional thanks to Coi Drummond-Gehrig, photo editor at the Denver Public Library Western History Department, for her extensive efforts in providing historic photos for the book. I'm also grateful to my longtime associate and mentor Dr. Tom Noel, whose comprehensive knowledge of Colorado history greatly improved the manuscript. Reviewers Mitch Benedict, Mark Flynn, Rod Greiner, Joseph Hodges, Jr., Carl Lindsay, Karen Lindsay, Darlene Mast, Jim McGibney, Doug McLemore, John Klug, Charlie Miller, and Seth Patterson very graciously shared their knowledge of club and local history. I'd also like to acknowledge Rotarian Bill Hornby, whose 75th Anniversary publication *A Club and the City*, and subsequent update helped provide context and background information for this book. Rotary International has been wonderful in providing information and photographs lacking from the club's archives.

Although time and space constraints prevented the inclusion of many interesting stories, I tried to capture the essence of Denver Rotary Club and its evolution through the decades. During the process, I was amazed to discover how influential Club 31 has been in Denver's history and the broad international scope of more recent efforts. In my opinion, the city and the world community owe a substantial debt of gratitude to this organization and its individual members for contributions to society too numerous to mention.

Hopefully, the 100th Anniversary celebration will inspire a resurgence of interest in the club's history so that any omissions from this document can be recorded and included in Denver Rotary archives for the 125th Anniversary celebration. Meanwhile, I've truly enjoyed meeting and working with all of you.

Happy Anniversary, Denver Rotary Club 31! You've made a great start!

Rosemary Fetter, Author

Congratulations to Rotary Club 31 on your 100th Anniversary!

Well Done!!

From your fellow Centenarian, The 106 year old National Western!

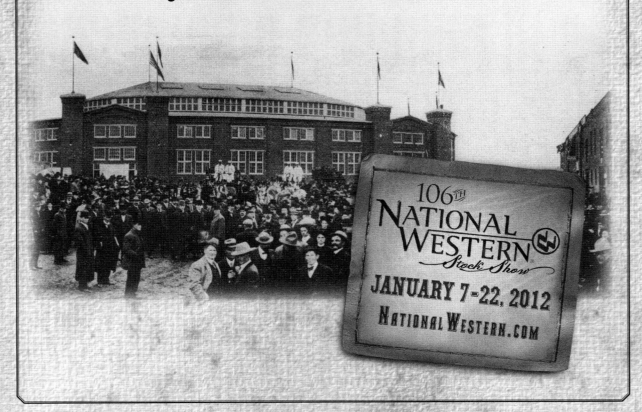

CenturyLink™

Qwest's longstanding commitment to our communities is demonstrated through our support for education programs, by maintaining a diverse workforce, and by protecting our environment through "green" initiatives. Serving communities is the legacy cornerstone of our business and we will continue to support public service programs that make our communities great places now and help ensure they remain that way in the future.

Roland Thornton
Executive Vice President of Wholesale Markets, Qwest, 2004–present

Floyd P. Ogden
President, Mountain States Telephone and Telegraph, 1943–1952

Walter Koch
President, Mountain States Telephone and Telegraph, 1952–1966

Lowell F. Wingert
President, Mountain States Telephone and Telegraph, 1966–1970

Robert K. Timothy
President, Mountain States Telephone and Telegraph, 1970–1983

Dwight D. Phelps
Vice President of Marketing, 1962–1970

Rotary stories have shaped who we have become; through one hundred years we have communicated our ideas and passions. They have helped define us; empower us, teach us through the mirror of the past. Our future is vibrant due to those who have gone before us and to the lessons wrought by the Rotary legacy.

Yours in Rotary,

Suzanne and William Hornby

INDEX

ABOUT THE AUTHOR

Rosemary Fetter is a Denver native with a lifelong love of local history. A graduate of the University of Colorado at Boulder, she was a social worker for several years. Following a career change, she became publications coordinator, and then public relations director at the Auraria Higher Education Center. While a graduate student in Colorado history at the University of Colorado at Denver, she wrote publications for the 1993 Colorado Woman's Suffrage Centennial Celebration and also administered the Golda Meir Museum for the campus. Since retiring from Auraria, she works as a freelance writer and part-time reporter for Villager Newspaper Publications.

Rosemary has published articles in *The Denver Post*; *The Rocky Mountain News*; *Colorado Expression*; *Architecture and Design of the West*; *Colorado Homes and Lifestyles*; *Colorado Heritage*; *University of Denver Magazine*; *Historic Denver News*; *Confetti*; and other publications. She has also written three other books, including histories of Graland Country Day School and Colorado Academy. Her second book, *Colorado's Legendary Lovers*, tells the story of famous couples in Colorado history.

A longtime member of the Denver Woman's Press Club, she has won in-house writing awards for nonfiction and commercial publications. Her interests include architecture, film and theater, antique ephemera, and the Italian language and culture. She loves travel, swimming, reading mysteries, her grandsons, and the history of just about anything.

Rotary International Clubs In District 113.
February 1, 1939

GOODLAND, KAN. 1925

BURLINGTON, COLO. 1936

PUEBLO, COLO. 1912

SALIDA, COLO. 1936

MONTE VISTA, COLO. 1920

CANON CITY, COLO. 1929

CREEDE, COLO. 1937

COSTILLA CO, COLO. 1937

ALAMOSA, COLO. 1923

DURANGO, COLO. 1929

SILVERTON, COLO. 1937

OURAY, COLO. 1938

LA JUNTA, COLO. 1920

ROCKY FORD, COLO. 1926

DEL. NORTE, COLO. 1930

LA JARA, COLO. 1930

CORTEZ, COLO. 1936

LAMAR, COLO. 1921

DENVER, COLO. 1911

COLO. SPRINGS, COLO. 1916

LIMON, COLO. 1937

LOVELAND, COLO. 1920

JOHNSTOWN, COLO. 1937

ENGLEWOOD, COLO. 1937

CASPER, WYO. 1919

LITTLETON, COLO. 1922

TORRINGTON, WYO. 1931

MORRILL, NEB. 1938

FT. MORGAN, COLO. 1936

CHEYENNE, WYO. 1918

LARAMIE, WYO. 1920

EATON, COLO. 1931

RAWLINS, WYO. 1921

LANDER, WYO. 1938

SHERIDAN, WYO. 1919

BUFFALO, WYO. 1925

BASIN, WYO. 1938

ESTES PARK, COLO. 1926

STERLING, COLO. 1920

WRAY, COLO. 1937

BRIGHTON, COLO. 1935

GREELEY, COLO. 1917

FT LUPTON, COLO. 1937

FT. COLLINS, COLO. 1918

GRAND JCT, COLO. 1919

OLATHE, COLO. 1937

MONTROSE, COLO. 1921

BOULDER, COLO. 1919

CLAYTON, N. MEX. 1918

LONGMONT, COLO. 1919

RATON, N. MEX. 1919

GUNNISON, COLO. 1922

TRINIDAD, COLO. 1919

FRUITA, COLO. 1936

WALSENBURG, COLO. 1925

LA VETA, COLO. 1937

DELTA, COLO. 1921

PAONIA, COLO. 1922

LINCOLN, NEB. 1910

SCOTTS BLUFF, NEB. 1920